Four Seasons

WITH POTATOES

THE potatoes from Britain's farms help provide complete, attractive and nourishing meals for all seasons of the year. In early summer the new potatoes, delicious and fresh flavoured, are harvested and rushed to the shops. They can, and should be on the dinner plates within twenty-four hours of lifting from the earth. It is only in their real freshness that the delicacy of taste can best be appreciated.

In the autumn the later maturing varieties become available. They are still fresh flavoured and rich in vitamin C but in being more mature they are much more versatile. With a little ingenuity they can be presented at table in dozens of appetising ways.

It is also in the autumn when the maincrop, long-keeping varieties of potatoes, are harvested and put into store and these ensure that we are well fed through the winter and spring months ahead.

Here in this book is a wide selection of attractive recipes especially chosen for each season of the year. Every one has been thoroughly tested. All are practical and if you are looking for ideas for economical meals you will find them in the following pages.

Accompanying each book is a useful wall chart which shows the varieties of potatoes most commonly available in Britain with their cooking qualities evaluated.

The book itself has been garnished with extracts and pictures from that delightful magazine "The Countryman". Why?

Just to give you pleasure in dipping into it whilst you choose some new and exciting ways in which to serve the potatoes from Britain's countryside.

Introduction
Crispin Gill
(Editor of *The Countryman*)

Crispin Gill and his wife Betty in the entrance hall of the editorial offices

THE first Englishman to describe the potato, John Sparke of Plymouth, a fellow townsman of mine, wrote 'these potatoes be the most delicate roots that may be eaten . . .' But how was it cooked, there on a West Indian beach 415 years ago, after this boy on his first voyage had bartered beads 'and other trifles' for this novel vegetable? A beach fire perhaps, of driftwood, with John Hawkins's young officers watching the naked Indians plucking baked potatoes from the ashes. It is as epic a moment in history as when Drake, silent upon that peak in Darien, first of all Englishmen beheld the Pacific.

What years of culinary discovery were to follow, from baked to boiled to roast, to the ubiquitous chip, to the elegant sophistication of this book.

Whole nations have survived on 'these delicate roots'. It has become the staple diet of these islands. For countrymen its cultivation has become a ritual: plant the first earlies on Good Friday, lift on Whit Monday. And whatever the effete townsman may do, no self-respecting countryman will look at a main course in a meal without its proper accompaniment of potatoes.

Nearly fifty years ago an article by a doctor in *The Countryman* spoke up for the true nutritional value of the potato, and not only quoted the experiment in which a man lived for eleven months entirely upon potatoes and vegetable margarine, with a flavouring of onion, but argued that these unorthodox ideas about diet were bringing down the Danish death rate.

No one is proposing such a diet today, but this book demonstrates that there is no need to be dull with the potato. Not only does it provide a variety of dishes but it takes a modern look at nutritional values and even, glory be, provides a diet on which one can both eat potatoes and slim. For years we have been told that if we would reduce we must eschew the noble tatie: now we can not only eat it but keep our weight down as well. For many of us this is as superb a discovery as young John Sparke made those centuries ago, for which I will gladly tender all my beads, pewter, whistles, glasses, knives and other trifles.

The Potato Marketing Board acknowledges with gratitude the facilities provided by "The Countryman" enabling a selection to be made of drawings, photographs, verse and other items which have appeared in the magazine and for the permission of the Editor to reproduce these in this book.

THE RECIPES

The recipes in this book were chosen from the register of more than 800 potato dishes maintained in the Potato Marketing Board's Test and Experimental Kitchen. Many were specially devised for this publication by the Board's Home Economists.

NUTRITIVE VALUE OF THE POTATO

Contribution of Potatoes to the Nutrient and Energy Intake from Fresh Potatoes in the Home*

National averages from Annual Report of National Food Survey Committee 1973

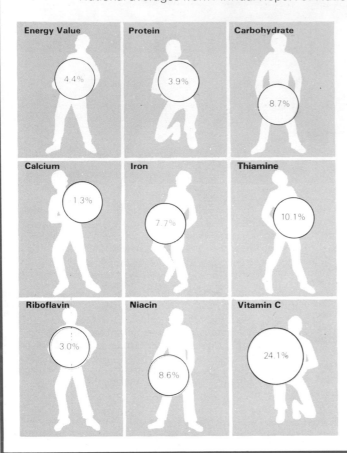

Energy Value — 4.4%
Protein — 3.9%
Carbohydrate — 8.7%
Calcium — 1.3%
Iron — 7.7%
Thiamine — 10.1%
Riboflavin — 3.0%
Niacin — 8.6%
Vitamin C — 24.1%

On average we eat more than 200 lb of potatoes annually and they hold a unique place in our diet. Nothing is regarded quite like them for providing a well balanced meal.

Contrary to popular belief potatoes are not a particularly fattening food and only become so when eaten in very large quantities or cooked in fat or oil.

The biological value of potato protein is very high, higher than any other plant protein and nearly as high as egg protein. Potatoes are the most important source of vitamin C in the British diet and they provide a valuable contribution to our requirements for vitamin B, iron and other essential nutrients.

Potatoes do not cause dental decay to the extent that other carbohydrate foods can do; they may provide some protection against coronary thrombosis.

*Based on consumption of 1.340kg eaten in the home weekly and expressed as percentages. Potatoes eaten outside the home are not included.

SLIMMING AND POTATOES

Carbohydrate, fat and protein provide energy. This is expressed as calories (kcals).

To keep a steady weight keep a steady balance between total calorific intake and energy used daily.

Count your calories carefully to stay slim and keep fit.

Potatoes are comparatively low in calories when served boiled or jacket baked.

Calories — Average Daily Requirement

	9/11 yrs	12/14 yrs	15/18 yrs	Adults—dep. on age & activity	
Children					
Girls	2300	2300	2300	Women	2200/2500
Boys	2500	2800	3000	Men	2700/3600

Calories Compared 100g portions

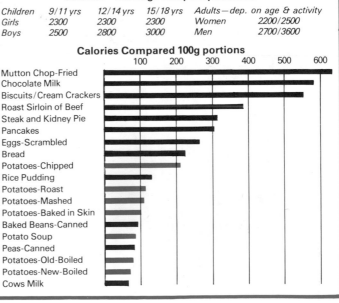

100 200 300 400 500 600

Mutton Chop-Fried
Chocolate Milk
Biscuits/Cream Crackers
Roast Sirloin of Beef
Steak and Kidney Pie
Pancakes
Eggs-Scrambled
Bread
Potatoes-Chipped
Rice Pudding
Potatoes-Roast
Potatoes-Mashed
Potatoes-Baked in Skin
Baked Beans-Canned
Potato Soup
Peas-Canned
Potatoes-Old-Boiled
Potatoes-New-Boiled
Cows Milk

Summer

"All twinkling with the dewdrop's sheen The briar-rose falls in streamer's green."
Scott

The Festive Ring

Serves 4

2 salt herring fillets
or 1 × 6 oz can herring fillets
6 oz new potatoes cooked and diced
3 baby beetroots, cooked and diced
1 red eating apple, unpeeled but diced
1 small onion, finely chopped
4 tablespoons beetroot juice
2 tablespoons hot water
2 level teaspoons sugar
pepper
2 teaspoons gelatine
2 tablespoons water
¼ pint double cream, whipped
2 eggs, hardboiled
watercress

Drain skin and dice the fish.
Mix with the potatoes, beetroots, apple and onion.
Blend the beetroot juice, water, sugar and pepper together and add to the fish mixture.
Dissolve the gelatine in the water and stir this into the cream, which should be carefully folded into the fish mixture.
Pack into a 7'' ring mould. Chill
Unmould and garnish with egg slices and watercress.

Photo page 6

Rosy Salad

Serves 4

8 oz cooked ham, cubed
1 lb new potatoes, cooked and diced
2 red eating apples, unpeeled but cored and diced
1 stick celery, sliced
1 oz seedless raisins
1 teaspoon chives, chopped
2 tablespoons natural yoghurt
1 tablespoon mayonnaise
generous pinch curry powder
finely shredded lettuce

Mix all the ingredients together except the lettuce.
Allow to stand for one hour.
Line a salad bowl with lettuce and arrange the potato mixture in the centre.
Serve immediately.

Photo page 6

Picture shows: Rosy Salad, Festive Ring, Celebration Chicken *(page 8)*.

Celebration Chicken

Serves 4

2 oz butter
4 chicken portions
1 lb new potatoes
¼ pint sherry
¼ pint double cream
½ teaspoon paprika pepper
1 clove of garlic, crushed
4 oz cheddar cheese, grated
1 teaspoon parsley, chopped

Melt the butter and fry the chicken portions for about 5 minutes until golden. Remove from the pan. Fry the potatoes until lightly golden. Remove from the pan, pour off the pan juices.

Replace the chicken in the pan flesh side down and pour the sherry over the chicken.

Top with a tightly fitting lid or aluminium foil and simmer for 30 minutes. Add the potatoes and simmer for a further 25 minutes.

Whip the cream quite stiffly and fold in the paprika pepper, garlic and cheese. Season with salt and pepper.

Transfer the chicken and potato mixture to an oven-proof serving dish.

Gently cover with the cheese topping and place under a hot grill until the cheese melts and turns golden.

Garnish with chopped parsley.

Photo page 6

Curried New Potato Scramble

Serves 4

1 lb new potatoes, cooked and diced
1 small onion, finely chopped
1 oz butter
1 teaspoon curry powder
4 eggs
⅓ pt milk
1 teaspoon parsley, chopped
salt and pepper

Fry the onion and the potatoes in the butter until the onion is soft and transparent.

Add the curry powder and fry slowly for 5 minutes stirring occasionally.

Beat the eggs, milk, parsley and seasoning and pour into the pan stirring gently until the mixture is scrambled.

Singapore Chicken

Serves 4

4 chicken quarters
1 oz seasoned flour
1 oz butter
1 lb small new potatoes
1 large onion
1 teaspoon ground ginger
2 tablespoons clear honey
1 × 15 oz can crushed
   pineapple
1 oz cornflour
½ pint chicken stock made
   with 1 whole stock cube
salt and pepper

Toss the chicken quarters in the seasoned flour and fry in the butter until lightly browned.

Transfer to a shallow casserole and arrange the potatoes between the chicken pieces.

Chop the onion and sauté in the butter until transparent. Stir in the ginger, honey and the pineapple.

Blend the cornflour with the stock and add to the onion mixture. Adjust the seasoning and bring to the boil.

Pour the sauce over the chicken and potatoes.

Cover and cook at 350°F (180°C) Gas Mark 4 for one hour.

Asparagus Potato and Salmon Cream

Serves 4

1 × 10 oz can green asparagus spears
2 teaspoons powdered gelatine
1 × 5 fl oz carton soured cream
4 tablespoons mayonnaise
2 tablespoons onion, finely chopped
salt and pepper
12 oz new potatoes, cooked and
    diced
2 eggs, hardboiled and chopped
1 × 7 oz can of salmon, drained and
    flaked
parsley, chopped

Drain the asparagus, reserving the liquor. Cut off the stalks and chop roughly. Reserve the tips for garnish.
Dissolve the gelatine in the asparagus liquor in a bowl held over a pan of hot water. Remove and cool.
Mix the cream, mayonnaise, onion and seasoning together, then pour in the dissolved gelatine stirring the mixture as you do so. Add the potatoes, eggs, salmon and chopped asparagus.
Pour into a greased fish mould and leave to set.
Turn out and decorate with asparagus tips and parsley.

Piquant Macquereau

Serves 4

4 smoked mackerel fillets
salt and freshly ground black pepper
1 lb new potatoes
2 large onions
2 tablespoons oil
2 tablespoons parsley finely chopped
2 tablespoons white breadcrumbs
2 oz butter
¼ pt single cream
juice of 1 lemon
lemon slices for garnishing

Season the fillets with salt and pepper.
Scrape and slice the potatoes. Peel and slice the onions and divide into rings.
Heat the oil in a frying pan and fry the onion rings over a low heat until they are soft and transparent.
Layer the fish, the potatoes, the onions and the parsley in a well buttered baking dish.
Sprinkle the breadcrumbs over the top and dot with butter. Cook at 375°F (190°C) Gas Mark 5 for 30 minutes.
Heat the cream gently in a saucepan, then pour it over the fish. Lastly, sprinkle the dish with lemon juice.
Serve immediately, garnished with twists of lemon.

Tongue Salad Mould

Serves 4

8 oz sliced tongue
2 level teaspoons gelatine
1 tablespoon water
3 tablespoons mayonnaise
1½ lb new potatoes, cooked and
    diced
1 small onion, grated
3 gherkins or olives, chopped
1 teaspoon parsley, chopped
salt and pepper
1 egg, hardboiled and sliced

Line an 8″ × 4″ loaf tin with greaseproof paper, extending the paper about 2 inches above the rim.
Line the tin with slices of tongue then dice the remainder.
Dissolve the gelatine in water. Mix the dissolved gelatine with the mayonnaise and pour this over the potatoes. Carefully fold the onions, gherkins or olives, parsley and seasoning into the potato mixture.
Place half the mixture into the tin, cover with diced tongue, then pour in the remainder of the potato mixture. Level off the top and fold paper over. Chill.
Before serving unfold the paper and turn the mould out onto a serving dish. Remove the lining paper.
Garnish with the sliced hardboiled egg.

Sugar Browned Potatoes

Serves 4

1 lb new potatoes, scraped
1 teaspoon salt
1 oz butter
1 oz sugar

Plunge the potatoes into boiling salted water. Return to boiling point then simmer for 15-20 minutes depending on size. Drain.

Melt the butter and sugar in the pan; add the potatoes and toss them over and over until they are golden brown.

Photo page 11

Vichysoisse

Serves 4

1 lb leeks, trimmed
8 oz potatoes, peeled and chopped
2 oz butter
1½ pints white stock
salt and pepper
3 tablespoons single cream
4 tablespoons white wine
chopped parsley and chives to
  garnish

Wash and slice the leeks.

Melt the butter and fry the leeks and potatoes gently for 10 minutes.

Add stock and seasoning to the pan and simmer for 20-25 minutes until the vegetables are tender.

Pass through a sieve or liquidiser.

Blend the cream and wine into the soup, then chill thoroughly.

Serve cold garnished with parsley and chives.

Photo Page 11

Stuffed Peppers

Serves 4

2 red peppers ⟩ approximately 4 oz
2 green peppers ⟩ in weight each
6 oz cream cheese
8 oz new potatoes cooked and diced
chives, chopped
parsley, chopped
salt and pepper
watercress

Cut away a thin slice from the stem end of each pepper. Remove core and seeds and wash.

Blend together all the other ingredients except the watercress.

Stuff the mixture into the peppers, packing firmly.

Chill for about 30 minutes.

Cut the peppers into quarters and serve on a bed of watercress.

Photo page 11

Summer Lamb Casserole

Serves 4

2 lb neck of lamb
½ pint stock
salt and pepper
1 tablespoon tomato purée
1 lb small new carrots
1 lb small new potatoes, scrubbed
  or scraped
8 oz fresh peas, shelled weight
chopped fresh mint for garnishing

Place the meat in a casserole with the stock and seasoning.

Cover and cook at 325°F (170°C) Gas Mark 3 for 2 hours. Remove and stir in the tomato purée.

Surround the meat with the carrots, potatoes and peas and put back into the oven for a further 30 minutes.

Garnish with chopped mint.

Photo page 11

Picture shows: Stuffed Peppers, Summer Lamb Casserole, Vichysoisse, Sugar Browned Potatoes ▶

Minted New Potato Salad

Serves 4

1 lb new potatoes, scrubbed
1 teaspoon salt
1 × 5 fl oz carton natural yoghurt
1 tablespoon fresh mint leaves,
  finely chopped
¼ teaspoon made mustard
pepper
1 tablespoon caster sugar
lettuce leaves

Plunge the potatoes into salted boiling water. Return to boiling point then simmer for 15-20 minutes depending on size, until cooked. Drain.

Make up the dressing by blending together the yoghurt, mint leaves, mustard, pepper and sugar.

Dice the potatoes and place in the bowl with the dressing. Blend gently together.

Chill before serving on a bed of lettuce.

Smoked Mackerel with New Potatoes

Serves 4

4 smoked mackerel fillets
¼ pint dry white wine
2 teaspoons lemon juice
2 teaspoons grated orange rind
1 lb new potatoes, cooked and
  sliced
1 oz butter

Place the mackerel in a shallow lightly greased baking dish.

Combine the wine, lemon juice and orange rind and pour over the fish.

Arrange the potatoes on top of the fish overlapping the slices as you do so. Dot with butter and bake at 375°F (190°C) Gas Mark 5 for 20 minutes.

Kingfisher

I'm a weed

I'm a weed, I'm a weed,
One of the old untameable breed;
I never came from a packet of seed.

I am no cossetted nursery child,
Nobody keeps my pedigree filed,
I am wild, I am wild, I am wild!

Do you think, sister Pink,
That it's nice to line borders on somebody's orders?
  The man who kindly plants you,
  When he no longer wants you
  Will throw you out to rot.

Won't you speak, Mr. Leek?
Do you like being made to stand stiffly on parade?
  He'll never let you flower
  Who has you in his power;
  He'll boil you in a pot.

New Potatoes in Lemon Sauce

Serves 4

½ oz butter
½ oz flour
¼ pt milk
¼ pt chicken stock
rind of a small lemon
juice of ½ small lemon
1 teaspoon sugar
salt and pepper
1 lb new potatoes, boiled
1 tablespoon single cream
1 tablespoon chopped parsley

Make the sauce by melting the butter, adding the flour and cooking for one minute. Gradually add the stock and milk stirring constantly until the sauce is smooth.

Add the lemon rind, lemon juice, sugar, salt, pepper and cooked potatoes to the pan and continue to simmer for 10 minutes.

Just before serving add the cream, shaking the pan gently to avoid breaking the potatoes.

Turn into serving dish and sprinkle with the chopped parsley.

Summer Tail Corn

OLD FARMER to his wife, on first seeing the sea, 'Look ee there Martha there be aacres and aacres on it!'

WILD LIFE. An old lady who had seen a cinema show—a natural history picture—said to her companion, 'What kinds of birds were they?' 'I don't really know', said her friend. 'No, I don't know either: at first I thought they were cuckoos but when I saw the eggs I knew they weren't cuckoos because they don't lay their own eggs'.

Can I suppose, Lady Rose,
  That you actually enjoy being treated like a toy,
    While they play genetic games on you,
    And stick their fancy names on you,
  Caught in a breeder's plot?

Freely I scatter my prodigal seeds;
Sun, wind and rain will provide for their needs.
Man cannot always be digging and hoeing,
While he's asleep, I get on with my growing.

I don't expect mercy, I won't ask for pardon,
And when you're all dead, I'll take over the garden.

T. R. Milford

Illustrated by Dennis Mallet

Bonfire

The bonfire that I lit last night
This morning shammed as dead;
And then I saw the single thread
Of smoke curl up, wavering, white,
From the half-burnt-out bed.

Then the wind caught it: flags of fire
Burst open on the summer air
Became a Phoenix bird in flight
In whose revival I could share
A dazzled new delight.

Douglas Gibson

SWEET REASON. My father, a notable vegetable grower, once found the beginnings of a mole's excavations on his brassica patch. Having dug down and located the mole's tunnel, and seeing a gardener friend coming down the path, he maintained his kneeling position and began to talk down the hole: 'Now see here, Mister Mole, I don't *want* to kill you, but if you come on my garden again I'll have you. So be warned, keep off!' His friend laughingly asked him what on earth he was up to. Assuming a straight face, which must have cost him much in self-control, my father repeated his mole-message. Needless to say, my father's friend treated it as a splendid joke—but the curious thing is that the mole never did return to that particular brassica patch.

Anthony Wootton, Buckinghamshire.

13

Summertime Hotpot

Serves 4

2 courgettes, topped and tailed
salt
1 oz butter
1 onion, chopped
1 clove garlic, crushed
12 oz new potatoes, scrubbed and
　　diced
8 oz button mushrooms
1 × 15 oz can apricot halves
2 oz salted peanuts
1 tablespoon cornflour
2 tablespoons redcurrant jelly
2 tablespoons red wine
1 tablespoon soy sauce
salt and pepper
4 bacon chops

Slice the courgettes ¼ inch thick. Sprinkle with salt and leave to drain.

Melt the butter and gently fry the onion, garlic and potatoes without browning.

Add the courgettes and mushrooms and simmer for approximately 10 minutes.

Drain the apricot halves, reserving the juice and add to the pan with the peanuts.

Blend the cornflour with the apricot juice, and pour into the pan along with the jelly, wine, soy sauce and seasoning.

Boil for a few minutes then turn into a large ovenproof dish.

Arrange the bacon chops on top and cook uncovered at 375°F (190°C) Gas Mark 5 for 45 minutes.

Lamb Chops de Luxe

Serves 4

½ oz Butter
8 small lamb chops
1 large onion, chopped
3 sticks celery, sliced
1 × 15 oz can apricot halves
salt and pepper
1 lb new potatoes, scraped

Melt the butter and fry the lamb chops on both sides until lightly browned. Transfer to a shallow casserole dish.

Lightly fry the onion and celery in the same fat until soft. Drain the apricot juice into the pan and mix with the pan juices. Season.

Arrange the potatoes amongst the chops and pour the contents of the saucepan over the top.

Cover and cook at 350°F (180°C) Gas Mark 4 for 45 minutes.

Make a border of apricot halves round the dish and return to the oven for another 15 minutes.

Serve accompanied by redcurrant jelly.

Hot Frankfurter Salad

Serves 4

1½ lb new potatoes
12 oz frankfurters
1 medium onion
6 tablespoons mayonnaise
2 tablespoons natural yoghurt
1 teaspoon made mustard
salt and pepper
parsley, chopped

Cut the new potatoes into ½ inch dice and plunge into boiling salted water for about 10 minutes until cooked. Drain.

Grill the sausages and cut each sausage into 6 pieces.

Chop the onion very finely.

Blend the mayonnaise, yoghurt, mustard, onion and seasoning together.

Toss the hot potatoes and sausages in this dressing.

Garnish with chopped parsley and serve immediately.

Crispy Potatoes

Serves 4

1 lb new potatoes, scraped
1 teaspoon salt
1½ oz butter
3 oz Parmesan cheese, grated

Plunge the potatoes into boiling salted water, allow the water to return to the boil then reduce the heat and continue to simmer for 15-20 minutes depending on the size of the potatoes. Drain.

Melt the butter in a pan and toss the potatoes in it until they are thoroughly coated.

Place the cheese in a plastic bag. Taking a few potatoes at a time shake them in the bag until they are covered with cheese.

Lay them on a lightly greased baking tray and crisp in the oven at 400°F (200°C) Gas Mark 6 for approximately 10 minutes until they are golden brown.

Pork Chop Casserole

'Serves 4

3 oz butter
8 oz onions, sliced
salt and pepper
1 teaspoon dry mustard
2 teaspoons soft brown sugar
4 pork chops
1 tablespoon flour
3 large oranges
¼ pt dry white wine
1 lb new potatoes, scraped

Heat 1 oz butter and fry the onions until golden brown. Remove from pan.

Melt the remaining 2 oz butter along with the salt, pepper, mustard and sugar. Fry the chops on both sides until golden brown. Remove from the pan.

Stir the flour into the pan juices. Add the rind from 2 oranges, also the onions.

Squeeze the juice from 2 oranges and make up to ¼ pint with water. Pour this into the pan stirring vigorously. Add the wine and bring the sauce to the boil. Leave to simmer.

Peel the remaining orange and divide into segments.

Place the potatoes in a greased casserole. Arrange the chops and the orange segments on top and cover with the sauce.

Cover and cook in the oven at 350° F (180°C) Gas Mark 4 for 1 hour.

Growing Crop

In the early days of summer you will see fields of growing potatoes almost everywhere in Britain. The very early potatoes come from Cornwall, Pembrokeshire, Kent and the south west coast of Scotland. Lincolnshire, Yorkshire, Essex and the eastern regions of Scotland produce the bulk of the maincrop potatoes and it is also in Scotland where seed potatoes of high quality are grown. These seed potatoes are needed for planting the following spring to produce the next year's crops. Many tonnes are exported and Scottish seed potatoes are held in high regard all over the world.

Banana and Grape Salad

Serves 4

8 oz cooked chicken
8 oz new potatoes, cooked
4 oz green grapes
1 small red pepper
2 small bananas
2 tablespoons mild mayonnaise
2 tablespoons double cream
salt and pepper
lettuce leaves

Dice the chicken and the new potatoes.

Skin and depip the grapes, deseed and chop the pepper, skin and slice the bananas.

Blend the cream and mayonnaise together to make the dressing then carefully fold in the other ingredients.

Season and serve on a bed of lettuce.

Unlike most potato salads which should be left to stand to absorb the flavours this salad should be served right away, otherwise the bananas tend to discolour.

Potato Paté

Serves 4

12 oz liver sausage
1 teaspoon onion, finely chopped
2 tablespoons mayonnaise
2 tablespoons double cream
1 teaspoon brandy or lemon juice
8 oz new potatoes, cooked and diced

Soften the liver sausage by beating well with a wooden spoon.

Add all the other ingredients with the exception of the potatoes and beat for a full minute until the mixture looks smooth and creamy. Gently mix in the potatoes.

Cover with foil and refrigerate overnight.

Turn out and serve with a tomato and onion salad.

Elderflower champagne
Ingredients: Elderflowers, 10 or 12 heads
White wine vinegar, 2 tablespoons
White sugar, 2 lb.
Water, 3 gall.
Lemons, 2

Pick the heads when in full bloom and put in a bowl with the lemon juice, cut-up rind and sugar dissolved in hot water and vinegar. Add the cold water and leave for three days, occasionally giving a good stir. Strain into strong bottles, cork firmly and lay them on their sides. After about two weeks it should be sparkling and ready to drink.

Dormice

> "The ruddy haws now clothe the half-leaved thorn . . ."
>
> Grahame

Jacket Baked Potatoes

Serves 4

4 × 8 oz potatoes
4 oz butter
salt and pepper
chopped chives to garnish

Scrub the potatoes to remove earth. Dry.

Place on a baking sheet and cook at 425°F (220°C) Gas Mark 7 for 1-1½ hours until the skin feels papery and yet the potato is soft.

With a sharp knife make a deep cross on top of the potatoes and press firmly until all four points open out.

Season with salt and pepper and top with butter.

Garnish with chopped chives.

Photo page 18

Mimosa Bakes

Serves 4

4 × 8 oz ready baked potatoes
2 oz butter
salt and pepper
2 eggs, hard boiled
4 oz smoked bacon, crisply grilled
  and chopped

Cut the potatoes in half lengthwise.

Scoop out the flesh, season and mash with the butter.

Chop the whites of the eggs and add to the potatoes with the diced bacon.

Pile the mixture back into the potato shells and reheat in a hot oven.

Garnish with sieved egg yolks.

Photo page 18

Piccadilly Bakes

Serves 4

4 × 8 oz ready baked potatoes
1 oz butter
4 rashers unsmoked bacon, diced
4 pineapple rings, cut into chunks
1 red pepper, deseeded and chopped
salt and pepper

Melt the butter in a pan, add the bacon, pineapple and red pepper and sauté gently until cooked.

Cut the potatoes in half lengthwise. Scoop the flesh into a bowl, season and mash.

Add the bacon, pineapple and pepper mixture and mix with the potato flesh.

Pile back into the potato shells and reheat in a hot oven.

If desired a little of the red pepper may be reserved for use as a garnish.

Photo page 18

Picture shows: Jacket Baked Potatoes, Soufflé Baked Potatoes *(page 20),* Fishermen's Boats *(page 20),* Piccadilly Bakes, Mimosa Bakes, Guy Fawkes *(page 20),* Miss Muffet *(page 20).*

Miss Muffet

Serves 4

4 × 8 oz ready baked potatoes
5 oz curd or cream cheese
salt and pepper
8 gherkins
1 tablespoon chopped parsley
4 lemon butterflies

Cut the potatoes in half lengthwise.
Scoop out the flesh and mix with the cheese. Season.
Dice 6 of the gherkins and add to the potato mixture.
Pile back into the potato shells and reheat in a hot oven.
Garnish with the chopped parsley, the 2 remaining gherkins cut into strips and the lemon butterflies.

Photo page 18

Guy Fawkes

Serves 4

4 × 8 oz ready baked potatoes
1 oz butter
salt and pepper
4 oz rough pâté
8 stuffed olives, sliced

Cut the potatoes in half lengthwise.
Scoop out the flesh and mash with the butter. Season.
Blend the pâté in to the potato mixture and pile back into the potato shells.
Reheat in a hot oven, then garnish with the sliced stuffed olives.

Photo page 18

Soufflé Baked Potatoes

Serves 4

4 × 8 oz ready baked potatoes
salt and pepper
2 oz butter
1 tablespoon cream
2 egg whites, stiffly beaten
sprigs of parsley to garnish

Cut the potatoes in half lengthwise.
Scoop the flesh out into a bowl and mash with the salt and pepper, butter and cream.
Fold in the stiffly beaten egg whites and pile the mixture back into the potato skins.
Place in the oven and cook at 350°F (180°C) Gas Mark 4 for 20-25 minutes.
Garnish each potato with a sprig of parsley.

Fishermen's Boats

Serves 4

4 × 8 oz ready baked potatoes
8 oz plaice fillets
1 oz butter
3 oz mushrooms
1 tablespoon sherry
5 tablespoons double cream
salt and pepper
yolk of 1 egg
2 oz cheese, finely grated

When the potatoes are practically ready poach the plaice fillets in a little salted water for 5 minutes.
Melt the butter and gently fry the mushrooms.
Drain the fish, flake and add to the mushrooms along with the sherry and 3 tablespoons of the cream. Season with salt and pepper.
Remove the potatoes from the oven and slice the top of each potato lengthwise. Scoop out most of the flesh leaving only a thin lining of potato to keep the shell upright.
Divide the fish mixture between the shells.
Mash the potato flesh, season and beat in the remainder of the cream, the egg yolk and the cheese.
Place the mixture in a piping bag fitted with a No. 10 star nozzle and pipe over the fish, covering the tops of the potato shells.
Return to the oven for 15 minutes until the tops are golden brown.

Photo page 18

Casserole of Potatoes

Serves 4

1½ lb potatoes, peeled and thinly
  sliced
salt and pepper
2 tablespoons parsley, chopped
2 oz butter, melted
¼ pint milk

Fill a greased casserole with layers of potato slices, adding salt, pepper, parsley and melted butter between each layer.

Pour the milk over the contents of the casserole and cook at 350°F (180°C) Gas Mark 4 for 1 hour.

Photo page 2

Leek and Potato Soup

Serves 4

2 medium leeks, cleaned and
  chopped
1 medium onion, finely chopped
1 oz butter
8 oz potatoes, mashed
1½-2 pints chicken stock
salt and pepper
4 tablespoons single cream
1 tablespoon parsley, chopped

Fry the leeks and onion very gently in the butter until soft.

Mix the potatoes with the chicken stock; the less stock you use the thicker the soup.

Add the leeks and onion, season to taste and bring to the boil. Simmer for 15 minutes.

Pour into individual bowls and garnish each with a tablespoon of cream and a little chopped parsley before serving.

Making the most of autumn

The light stretches a long way today
pushing the clouds to other continents,
and fields look twice their size because the sun
touches horizons twenty miles away.

Black furrows merge towards a stranded house
shining like some small spider in its web;
potato-pickers on a distant farm
could be wildflowers bending in the wind.

A tractor pulls a parachute of gulls
to check its landing speed before it turns
to plough new flights of soil, while in the sky
larks make again a rainbow of bright sound.

And in backyards, or on some new estate,
greenhouses flash with rich chrysanthemums
giving the day such things to celebrate
that winter dares not come to spoil earth yet.

Edward Storey

Tears

Suffolk gardener "Reckon I set they taters too near to they onions, 'cos when I took up they first lot of taters they were wet eyed!"

Owl

Dice D'or Noisettes

Serves 4

4 noisettes of lamb
1 oz butter
1 tablespoon cooking oil

1 lb potatoes, cut into ½ inch cubes
1 clove garlic, crushed
1 oz butter
2 tablespoons cooking oil
salt and pepper

Sauce

2 oz butter
4 oz mushrooms, sliced
1 tablespoon shallots, chopped
1 oz flour
¼ pint white wine
½ pint chicken stock
1 teaspoon tomato purée
1 tablespoon tarragon, chopped
1 tablespoon cheveril, chopped
watercress for garnishing

Heat 1 oz butter and 1 tablespoon cooking oil in a frying pan and sauté the noisettes of lamb gently until cooked.

While they are cooking heat 1 oz butter and 2 tablespoons cooking oil in a shallow pan. Add the potatoes, garlic, salt and pepper and fry gently until soft and golden brown.

Make the sauce by frying the mushrooms and shallots gently in 1 oz of the butter. Remove the vegetables from the pan.

Add the remaining 1 oz butter to the pan and when melted add the flour, cooking until it is lightly browned.

Gradually add the wine and stock, then stir in the tomato purée.

Return the mushrooms and shallots to the pan along with the tarragon and cheveril. Bring to the boil and allow to simmer gently for 5 minutes.

To serve spoon the sauce over the noisettes placed in the centre of a serving dish and surround the meat with the potatoes.

Garnish with sprigs of watercress.

Photo page 2

Quick Potato Soup

Serves 4

1 lb potatoes, grated
1 large onion, grated
2 oz butter
1½ pints chicken stock
salt and pepper
¼ pint milk
4 oz Cheddar cheese, grated
pinch of nutmeg

Fry the vegetables gently in the melted butter.

Add the stock, salt and pepper. Bring to the boil, cover and simmer for 20 minutes.

Add the milk and reheat. Check the seasoning.

Serve topped with grated cheese and a dash of nutmeg.

Potato Royale

Serves 4

1 pheasant
2 oz seasoned flour
2 oz butter
3 medium onions, chopped
2 tablespoons sweet tomato chutney
¼ pint red wine
¼ pint chicken stock
salt and pepper
1½ lb potatoes, peeled and sliced

Cut the pheasant into small joints and toss in seasoned flour.

Fry in butter with the onions until lightly browned then place in a casserole.

Mix together the chutney, wine and stock and pour over the pheasant. Season with salt and pepper.

Lay the potatoes in overlapping slices over the contents of the casserole.

Cover with a close fitting lid or foil and cook at 325°F (170°C) Gas Mark 3 for 1½ hours. Uncover, increase the heat to 400°F (200°C) Gas Mark 6 and cook for a further 30 minutes to crisp and brown the potatoes.

Cover picture

Spinach and Potato Soup

Serves 4

2 oz butter
1 large onion, sliced
12 oz potatoes, peeled and diced
1½ pints chicken stock
1 lb frozen spinach
salt and pepper
½ pint single cream

Melt the butter and sauté the onion and potatoes gently until softened but not coloured. Shake the pan from time to time to prevent them sticking.

Add the stock, spinach, salt and pepper and cook for 15 minutes.

Sieve or liquidise and check the seasoning. Stir in the cream and reheat, but do not allow the soup to boil.

Argyll Soup

Serves 4

2 large carrots, quartered
2 large onions, quartered
4 stalks celery, chopped
1 lb potatoes, quartered
2 cloves garlic, crushed
salt and pepper
2 pints chicken stock

Put all the vegetables into a pan with the seasoning and stock.

Bring to the boil and skim if necessary.

Simmer for approximately 45 minutes until the vegetables are cooked.

Sieve or liquidise the soup. Check the seasoning and reheat.

Blackberrying *by Pamela Holmes*

Even for a child
Something nostalgic in it.
The wild
Untidy brambles,
Solitary lanes:
The buckled baskets
With last year's purple stains.

The busy silence
Under a September sky
Of fair and fragile blue:
We took the loot—
Concentration stemmed
Even our magpie chatter—
Baskets crammed
With the tiny fruit,
Bearing the peculiar blackberry bloom—
A dusky gleam.

Then, on the homeward troop, Father, chief pirate,
Bawdy, singing:
Shouting, touching-last,
Baskets brimming.
Into a sunset, smoky red,
One swallow winging.

Goldfinch

23

Cauliflower and Tomato Cheese

Serves 4

2 medium onions, chopped
1 oz butter
10 oz tomatoes, skinned and chopped
1 teaspoon basil
salt and pepper
1 lb potatoes, boiled and sliced
    ¼ inch thick
1 small cauliflower, cooked and
    divided into florets
4 oz Cheddar cheese, grated

Sauté the onions in the butter for about 10 minutes, until cooked but not coloured.

Add the tomatoes, basil, salt and pepper and simmer gently for 5 minutes.

Arrange the potato slices in the base of a greased casserole, cover with the well drained cauliflower and pour the tomato mixture over the vegetables.

Sprinkle the grated cheese over the contents of the casserole and cook at 400°F (200°C) Gas Mark 6 for 20 minutes until the cheese is a golden bubbly brown.

Potato Cheese Nibbles

Serves 4

1 lb potatoes, grated
4 oz Cheddar cheese, grated
2 oz self raising flour
2 eggs, beaten
salt and pepper
deep fat for frying
paprika pepper for garnishing

Squeeze all the excess water out of the potatoes.

Mix together all the ingredients and season to taste.

Drop small spoonfuls of the mixture into hot deep fat and fry until golden brown.

Drain on kitchen paper and dust with paprika pepper.

Cheese Croquettes

Serves 4

2 oz butter
2 oz flour
¼ pint milk
6 oz Cheddar cheese, grated
1 tablespoon parsley, chopped
pinch salt
dash of cayenne pepper
1 egg, separated
1 lb potatoes, boiled and sieved
browned breadcrumbs
deep fat for frying

Melt the butter in a saucepan, add the flour and cook for 1-2 minutes. Gradually add the milk stirring briskly.

Lower the heat, add the cheese, parsley, salt and cayenne pepper to the sauce, stirring well until the cheese has melted.

Remove from the heat, add the egg yolk and potatoes and beat until smooth.

Divide the mixture into 8 portions and roll into croquettes.

Beat the egg white lightly until frothy. Roll the croquettes in the egg white then in breadcrumbs.

Deep fry for 4-5 minutes until golden brown.

Savoury Cheese Pudding

Serves 4

4 oz Cheddar cheese, grated
2 eggs, hard boiled and chopped
1 lb potatoes, mashed
salt and pepper
1 large onion, chopped
1 oz butter
3 tomatoes, skinned and sliced

Add 2 oz of the cheese and the hard boiled eggs to the potatoes. Season.

Gently fry the onion in the butter until transparent, add the tomatoes and fry for a further minute.

Place half the potato mixture in a greased casserole.

Cover with the fried onions and tomatoes and top with the remainder of the potato mixture.

Scatter the remaining 2 oz cheese over the dish and bake at 425°F (220°C) Gas Mark 7 for 30 minutes.

Herb Delights

Serves 4

1 oz butter
salt and pepper
12 oz potatoes, boiled
3 eggs, separated
½ teaspoon mixed herbs
deep fat for frying

Over a low heat add the butter, salt and pepper to the potatoes and mash well.

Beat the egg yolks and mixed herbs into the mixture.

Whisk the egg whites until stiff and gently fold into the potatoes.

Drop dessertspoonfuls of the mixture into hot fat and fry until golden brown. Drain on kitchen paper.

Sausage Scallop

Serves 4

1 lb potatoes, peeled and thinly sliced
8 oz leeks chopped
1 lb sausages
salt and pepper
½ pint milk
2 oz white breadcrumbs

Arrange half the potatoes in the base of a greased casserole.

Scatter half the leeks over the potatoes and arrange the sausages on top of the vegetables. Toss the remaining leeks into the casserole and finish with a layer of overlapping sliced potatoes, seasoning as you go.

Pour the milk over the contents of the casserole and top with the breadcrumbs.

Cook at 375°F (190°C) Gas Mark 5 for 1¼ - 1½ hours until the potatoes are soft.

The farmhouse

In my mind's eye I clearly see
The farmhouse and the trees
That shaded it in summer months,
Then sprinkled it with leaves
During the splendid autumn days
When all the world was fair
To a boy who did not know then
That all his world was there.

Robert Brown

Strike a light

This comment appeared in an entry to the Common Scripture Examination of November 1974.
    "Lot's wife was a pillar of salt by day and a ball of fire by night."

Rev. L. J. Birch, Worcester.

Badger

Vegetable Sun Up

Serves 4

1 oz butter
1 lb potatoes, peeled and diced
1 lb tomatoes, skinned and sliced
1 green pepper, deseeded and
   chopped
1 clove garlic, crushed
salt and pepper
a little sugar if necessary
4 eggs, poached

Melt the butter in a saucepan and add the potatoes, tomatoes, green pepper, garlic, salt and pepper.

Cover with a lid and cook gently for 20 minutes shaking the pan occasionally to prevent the vegetables sticking.

When cooked check the seasoning, adding a little sugar if necessary.

Turn out onto a hot shallow serving dish and top with the poached eggs.

Note: – If the tomatoes are very ripe it may be necessary to reduce the liquid content by removing the saucepan lid and boiling briskly for the last few minutes of the cooking time.

Wiltshire Marrow

Serves 4

1 lb bacon pieces
1 tablespoon cooking oil
1 medium sized vegetable marrow,
   peeled and cubed
1 large onion, chopped
1 clove garlic, crushed
8 oz tomatoes, skinned and sliced
salt and pepper
1 lb potatoes, parboiled for 10 minutes
1 oz butter, melted

Fry the bacon pieces in the cooking oil until well browned. Transfer to a casserole.

Mix the marrow cubes with the bacon in the casserole.

Fry the onion and garlic gently until soft. Add the tomatoes to the onions and continue cooking for another few minutes. Season.

Spread the vegetables over the bacon and marrow pieces.

Slice the parboiled potatoes and cover the contents of the casserole with a layer of overlapping potato slices.

Brush the potatoes with melted butter and cook uncovered at 375°F (190°C) Gas Mark 5 for 40 minutes.

Carrot Cream Flan

Serves 4

Peanut Potato Pastry

4 oz potatoes, cooked and mashed
2 oz salted peanuts, finely ground
6 oz flour
1 teaspoon baking powder
2 oz butter
water to bind

Filling

2 eggs
¼ pint single cream
¼ pint milk
salt and pepper
8 oz potatoes, grated
8 oz carrots, coarsely grated
1 onion, finely chopped
2 tablespoons chutney
3 oz Cheddar cheese, grated

Make the pastry by creaming the butter and adding all the other ingredients, blending well together. Use as little water as possible to bind the pastry.

Knead on a floured board and mould into an 8″ flan ring.

Beat together the eggs, cream milk, salt and pepper.

Squeeze the excess water out of the potatoes and add to the egg mixture along with the carrots, onion and chutney, blending the ingredients well together. Spoon into the pastry case.

Scatter the cheese over the flan and bake at 400°F (200°C) Gas Mark 6 for 20 minutes. Reduce the heat to 350°F (180°C) Gas Mark 4 and continue cooking for a further 15-20 minutes.

Hot Potato Salad

Serves 4

1 onion, finely chopped
2 oz butter
12 oz potatoes, cooked
1 × 5 fluid oz. carton soured cream
salt and pepper
2 tablespoons parsley, chopped

Fry the onion in butter for 5 minutes without colouring.
Cut the potatoes into large dice and toss in the butter with the onions until the potatoes turn golden.
Stir in the soured cream and season. Add the parsley and cook gently until the cream bubbles.

Continental Potatoes

Serves 4

1¼ lb potatoes, peeled
1 onion, finely chopped
1 oz butter
1 tablespoon cooking oil
pinch of cumin, optional

Parboil the potatoes in salted water for 10 minutes, then cut into thin slices.
Fry the onion gently in the butter and oil, add the sliced potatoes and cumin and cook until the potatoes are brown on both sides. Drain off any excess fat before serving.

Mixed Vegetable Pie

Serves 4

1 large onion, sliced
2 oz butter
1 lb potatoes, mashed
1 lb cooked meat, minced
4 oz parsnips, mashed
4 oz carrots, mashed
¼ pint stock

Lightly fry the onion in 1 oz butter until soft and golden.
In the base of a greased ovenproof pie dish put a layer of mashed potatoes.
Cover this with alternating layers of meat, onion and vegetables, seasoning between each layer as you do so.
Moisten with the stock and top with the remaining mashed potatoes.
Dot the top with the remaining butter and place in a moderate oven.
Cook for 45 minutes at 350°F (180°C) Gas Mark 4 until the topping is crisp and brown.

Potato Harvesting

The bulk of Britain's potato crop is harvested in September and October. Nowadays much of the crop is lifted from the ground by large machines which separate the potatoes from the soil and stones. The Potato Marketing Board has encouraged the development of potato harvesters which can safely handle a crop, highly susceptible to damage, by organising biennial International Demonstrations. At these farmers can see and compare numerous machines and decide which will best suit the soil conditions on their farms.

Spanish Wedge

Serves 4

6 oz onions chopped
1 small green pepper, deseeded and
    chopped
1 clove garlic, crushed
1 oz butter
12 oz potatoes, cooked and diced
4 oz cooked ham, chopped
6 eggs
2 tablespoons water
salt and pepper

In a 9 inch frying pan fry the onions, pepper and garlic in the butter until soft, but not coloured.

Add the potatoes and ham and fry for another minute or two.

Whisk together the eggs, water salt and pepper and pour into the frying pan.

With a fork or a spatula swirl the mixture away from the sides of the pan.

When the underside is set place the pan under a hot grill to set the top.

Cut into four wedges and serve with a tossed green salad.

Lairds Flan

Serves 4

4 oz shortcrust pastry
2 eggs, beaten
¼ pint single cream
1 teaspoon made mustard
8 oz smoked haddock, cooked and
    flaked
4 oz potatoes, cooked and diced
pepper
1½ oz Cheddar cheese, grated

Line a 7'' flan tin with the pastry. Bake blind for 10 minutes at 400°F (200°C) Gas Mark 6.

Beat the eggs, cream and mustard together. Add the smoked haddock and potatoes and season with pepper.

Place this mixture in the pastry case, sprinkle with the cheese and bake at 350°F (180°C) Gas Mark 4 for 20-25 minutes until the egg has set and the cheese is a golden bubbly brown.

Shrimp Croquettes

Serves 4

2 egg yolks, beaten
1 × 6 oz can shrimps, chopped
2 tablespoons parsley, chopped
salt and pepper
1 lb potatoes, mashed
1 egg beaten
breadcrumbs
cooking oil for deep frying

Add the egg yolks, shrimps, parsley, salt and pepper to the potatoes and mix well together.

Shape into 12 rolls with floured hands. Roll in the beaten egg, then in the breadcrumbs.

Deep fry until golden brown, approximately 7 minutes.

Serve with a tossed green salad.

Smoked Haddock Fish Cakes

Serves 4

1 oz butter
1 oz flour
¼ pint milk
8 oz smoked haddock, cooked and
    flaked
8 oz potatoes, mashed
1 egg, beaten
breadcrumbs
cooking oil for frying

Make a sauce by melting the butter adding the flour and cooking for 1 minute. Stir in the milk beating well until it comes to the boil and the sauce thickens.

Bind the fish and potatoes with the sauce. Season.

Form the mixture into cakes ¾ inch thick. Dip into the beaten egg and then coat with breadcrumbs.

Shallow fry in hot fat for 5 minutes on each side until golden brown.

Creamy Rabbit Hotpotch

Serves 4

1 lb boned rabbit meat
1 oz seasoned flour
2 oz butter
4 oz lean bacon, diced
1 onion, chopped
8 oz carrots, cut into small dice
4 oz swede, cut into small dice
½ pint milk
½ pint chicken stock
salt and pepper
1½ lb potatoes, peeled and thinly
   sliced
1 tablespoon cooking oil
1 tablespoon parsley, chopped

Cut the rabbit into pieces and toss in the seasoned flour.

Melt the butter in a pan and fry the rabbit, bacon and onion for 5 minutes. Add the carrots and swede and continue cooking for a further 2-3 minutes.

Pour in the milk and stock and season with salt and pepper. Return to the boil then transfer the contents of the pan to a deep casserole.

Arrange the potato slices on top of the casserole. Sprinkle with a little salt and brush with the cooking oil.

Cover with a lid or foil and cook at 350°F (180°C) Gas Mark 4 for 1 hour. Remove the lid and cook for a further 30 minutes to crisp the potatoes.

Garnish with chopped parsley.

Potato Bourguignonne

Serves 4

1½ lb chuck steak, cut into 2 inch
   cubes
1 oz flour
1 oz butter
1 large onion, chopped
4 oz shoulder bacon, cut into ½ inch
   dice
4 oz mushrooms, chopped
1 teaspoon tomato purée
½ pint red wine
½ pint beef stock
bouquet garni
salt and pepper
1 lb potatoes, peeled and cut into
   chunks
chopped parsley for garnishing

Toss the steak in the flour. Melt the butter in a saucepan and brown the steak on all sides. Remove from the pan and place in a casserole.

Fry the onion, bacon and mushrooms gently for a few minutes.

Add the tomato purée, red wine, stock, bouquet garni, salt and pepper. Bring to the boil and pour over the meat.

Top with the potatoes and season again with salt and pepper.

Cover and cook for 2 hours at 350°F (180°C) Gas Mark 4.

Remove the bouquet garni and garnish with chopped parsley before serving.

Casserole of Beef

Serves 4

1 lb stewing steak, trimmed and cut
   into pieces
1 oz seasoned flour
1 oz butter
2 medium onions, peeled and
   sliced
1 lb potatoes, peeled and cut
   into chunks
4 oz carrots, peeled and sliced
1 bay leaf
2 tablespoons chutney
salt and pepper
¼ pint Guinness or stout
½ pint beef stock

Toss the steak in seasoned flour.

Melt the butter in a large pan. Fry the steak and onions until well browned.

Add the potatoes, carrots, bay leaf, chutney, salt and pepper, stout and stock.

Cover and simmer gently for 1½-2 hours. Remove the bay leaf and adjust the seasoning before serving.

Devilled Beef and Potatoes

Serves 4

1¼ lb stewing steak
1 oz seasoned flour
2 tablespoons cooking oil
1 large onion, sliced
½ pint stock
2 tablespoons tomato purée
1 teaspoon Worcestershire sauce
1 teaspoon English mustard
pinch cayenne pepper
1 small red pepper, deseeded and
    sliced
1 lb potatoes, peeled and sliced
1 tablespoon brandy, optional

Cube the stewing steak and toss in the seasoned flour.

Heat the oil and fry the meat and onion until well browned.

Add the stock, tomato purée, Worcestershire sauce, mustard and cayenne pepper. Simmer slowly for 1 hour.

Add the red pepper and potatoes, and cook for a further 30-40 minutes.

Just before serving pour in the brandy and check seasoning.

Plaice with Bananas

Serves 4

2 bananas
4 large plaice fillets, skinned
salt and pepper
¼ pint water
white wine
2 oz butter
1 oz flour
1 teaspoon grated lemon rind
1 egg, beaten
1 lb potatoes, cooked and sieved
1 tablespoon double cream
1 egg yolk
lemon slices to garnish

Cut the bananas in half crosswise and roll a fillet of fish round each banana.

Place in the centre of a fireproof dish, season with salt and pepper and cover with the water.

Poach in the oven for 15 minutes at 350°F (180°C) Gas Mark 4. Drain the liquor off carefully and make up to ½ pint with the wine. Keep the fish warm.

Make a sauce by melting 1 oz butter in a saucepan, stir in the flour and gradually add the wine/liquor and the lemon rind stirring all the time. Adjust the seasoning and bring to the boil, simmer for a few minutes.

Add 1 oz butter and beaten egg to the potatoes beating thoroughly. Place the potatoes in a piping bag fitted with a star nozzle and pipe a border of potatoes round the edge of a serving dish. Flash under a hot grill.

Arrange the banana fillets in the centre of the dish.

Remove the sauce from the heat, beat in the cream and egg yolk and spoon over the fish.

Garnish with lemon twists.

Atlantica

Serves 4

1 lb potatoes, cooked and sliced
    ¼ inch thick
3 eggs beaten
8 oz cottage cheese
1 × 7 oz can tuna fish, drained and
    flaked
salt and pepper
1 oz butter
1 tomato, sliced
few sprigs watercress

Line the base of a deep ovenproof dish with half of the potatoes.

Mix together the eggs, cottage cheese and tuna. Season well.

Pour the mixture into the dish and cover with the remaining potato slices.

Dot with butter and cook at 350°F (180°C) Gas Mark 4 for 30 minutes.

Garnish with tomato slices and watercress.

Chcviot Ring

Filling

1 lb shoulder lamb, cut into 1 inch cubes
1 oz seasoned flour
1 oz butter
1 large onion, chopped
1 large carrot, scraped and diced
1 × 8 oz can tomatoes
1 chicken stock cube
1 teaspoon rosemary, crushed
salt and pepper
1 × 5 fluid oz natural yoghurt

Potato Ring

¼ oz butter
1 oz browned breadcrumbs
2 lb potatoes, boiled
4 oz Cheddar cheese, grated
1 heaped tablespoon chopped chives

Toss the lamb in the seasoned flour and fry in the butter with the onion until well browned. Add the carrots and cook for a further 1-2 minutes.

Add the tomatoes, stock cube, rosemary, salt and pepper and bring to the boil.

Cover and simmer for 1-1½ hours until the meat is tender.

Grease a ring mould with the butter and sprinkle with breadcrumbs.

Mash the potatoes and beat in the cheese and chives. Place in the mould and press well down with the back of a spoon.

Bake at 400°F (200°C) Gas Mark 6 for 30 minutes. Turn out onto a serving plate and keep warm.

Remove the filling from the heat and stir in the yoghurt. Reheat slightly, but do not allow the mixture to reach boiling point.

Pile the filling into the centre of the potato ring allowing the juices to run down the sides of the ring.

Blue Tits

Beech Leaves

In autumn down the beechwood path
The leaves lie thick upon the ground;
It is there I love to kick my way
And hear their crisp and crashing sound.

I am a giant, and my steps
Echo and thunder to the sky.
How the small creatures of the wood
Must quake and cower as I pass by!

This brave and merry noise I make
In summer also, when I stride
Down to the shining pebbly sea,
And kick the frothing waves aside.

A. J. Reeves

Humpty Dumpties

Serves 4

1 lb potatoes, mashed
8 oz sausagemeat
1 tablespoon Worcestershire sauce
1 teaspoon made mustard
cooking oil for frying
2 oz red Cheshire cheese, grated
1 tablespoon parsley, chopped
8 tomato slices

Place the potatoes, sausagemeat, Worcestershire sauce and mustard in a bowl and beat until the ingredients are well blended.

Divide the mixture into 8 balls, then flatten into cakes.

Heat the oil and fry the cakes for approximately 5 minutes on each side.

Remove to an ovenproof plate.

Sprinkle each cake with grated cheese and flash under a very hot grill until the cheese bubbles and browns.

Garnish with chopped parsley and tomato slices.

Photo page 33

Chipolata Flan

Serves 6

Potato Pastry

3 oz butter
4 oz potatoes, mashed
5 oz plain flour
1 teaspoon baking powder

Filling

8 oz chipolata sausages, lightly grilled
2 eggs, beaten
¼ pint single cream
4 tablespoons milk
1 tablespoon tomato purée
pinch of nutmeg
salt and pepper

Make the pastry by creaming the butter until soft.

Add the potatoes, the flour and the baking powder and blend well together, without the addition of any other liquid.

Turn out onto a lightly floured board and roll out to fit an 8 inch flan tin or ring.

Cut the chipolates in half and arrange in the pastry case.

Whisk together the remaining ingredients and pour over the sausages.

Bake at 400°F (200°C) Gas Mark 6 for 10 minutes, reduce the heat to 350°F (180°C) Gas Mark 4 and continue baking for a further 25 minutes.

Photo page 33

Knight's Soup

Serves 4

8 oz potatoes, cut in large dice
1 lb tomatoes, skinned and sliced
3 oz carrots, diced
4 oz onions, sliced
½ teaspoon mixed herbs
2 pints chicken stock
salt and pepper
sugar to taste
2 tablespoons cream

Place the prepared vegetables in a large pan.

Add the herbs, stock, salt and pepper and bring to the boil. Simmer gently for 1½ hours.

Sieve or liquidise the soup and return to the pan. Check the seasoning, adding a little sugar if desired and reheat.

Serve with the cream swirled over the soup.

Photo page 33

Potato Lorraine

Serves 4

4 oz Cheddar cheese, grated
1 lb potatoes, cooked and sliced
2 eggs, beaten
¼ pint milk
pinch of nutmeg
salt and pepper
1 oz butter

Scatter half the cheese over the bottom of a greased pie dish.

Cover the cheese with the potato slices.

Beat the eggs, milk and nutmeg together and season well with salt and pepper. Pour over the potatoes.

Scatter the remaining cheese on top of the dish. Dot with butter and bake at 375°F (190°C) Gas Mark 5 for 30 minutes until golden bubbly brown.

Deerstalker's Stew Pot

Serves 4

1 oz fat for frying
1 lb stewing venison, cut into pieces
6 oz bacon, cut into ½ inch cubes
1 lb potatoes, peeled and cut into
    1 inch cubes
6 oz carrots, cut into fingers
8 oz onions, cut into quarters
¼ pint red wine
½ pint beef stock
salt and pepper
4 oz redcurrant jelly
1 dessertspoon cornflour

Heat the fat in a pan and quickly brown the venison and the bacon on all sides.

Add the potatoes, carrots, onions, wine, stock, salt and pepper.

Bring to the boil then simmer gently for 2 hours.

Add the redcurrant jelly and allow it to dissolve.

Thicken the gravy with the cornflour, check the seasoning and bring back to the boil before serving.

Photo page 33

Lamb and Cabbage Hotpot

Serves 4

1½ lb breast of lamb, cut into 1 inch
    cubes
1 oz seasoned flour
1 oz butter
1 lb white cabbage, shredded
3 stalks celery, chopped
salt and black pepper
½ pint stock
1 lb potatoes, peeled and sliced
    ¼ inch thick

Toss the lamb in seasoned flour and fry in the butter until the meat is sealed.

Place half the meat in the bottom of a casserole, follow with a layer of cabbage and top with celery. Sprinkle with salt and a generous shake of black pepper.

Repeat the three layers once more and season for a second time.

Overlap the potato slices on top of the meat and vegetables.

Pour in the stock.

Cover the dish tightly and cook at 350°F (180°C) Gas Mark 4 for 1¼ hours. Remove the lid, increase the heat to 425°F (220°C) Gas Mark 7 and continue cooking for another 30 minutes to brown the potatoes.

Lamb Bourganza

Serves 4

4 oz bacon, chopped
1 medium onion, sliced
1 clove garlic, crushed
4 oz button mushrooms
1½ lb stewing lamb
1 lb potatoes, peeled
1 oz flour
1 tablespoon tomato purée
¼ pint stock
¼ pint white wine
1 teaspoon sugar
salt and pepper
1 tablespoon parsley, chopped

Fry the bacon until crisp, remove from the frying pan.

Fry the onion, garlic and mushrooms in the bacon fat until soft but not coloured and then remove from the frying pan.

Cut the lamb and the potatoes into bite sized pieces. Toss the lamb in the flour and then fry with the potatoes for 5 minutes turning frequently until browned.

Return the bacon, onion, garlic and mushrooms to the pan along with the tomato purée, stock, wine, sugar and seasoning.

Bring to the boil and then turn into a casserole and cook at 350°F (180°C) Gas Mark 4 for 1¼ hours.

Adjust the thickening if necessary and scatter the parsley over the Bourganza before serving.

Country Pork and Bacon Loaf

Serves 4

1 oz butter
1 onion, chopped
2 celery sticks, chopped
8 oz pork sausagemeat
8 oz potatoes, mashed
2 tablespoons parsley, chopped
salt and pepper
2 egg yolks
4 oz streaky bacon, derinded

Melt the butter and fry the onion and celery gently for 5 minutes. Turn into a mixing bowl.

Combine the sausagemeat, mashed potatoes, parsley and seasoning with the onion and celery. Beat the egg yolks into the sausagemeat mixture.

Stretch the bacon rashers with the back of a round bladed knife and arrange across the base and sides of a greased loaf tin.

Turn the sausagemeat filling into the tin and press down well.

Cover the tin with foil and place in a baking tin half filled with hot water. Cook at 350°F (180°C) Gas Mark 4 for 1-1½ hours.

Jumbo Cakes

Serves 4

1½ lb potatoes, mashed
2 eggs, hard-boiled and finely chopped
4 oz cooked meat, cut into small dice
½ medium onion, grated
1 teaspoon tomato purée
1 tablespoon Worcestershire sauce
2 oz plain flour
salt and pepper
1 tablespoon cooking oil
1 oz butter
parsley sprigs

Thoroughly blend together the potatoes, eggs, cooked meat, onion, tomato purée, Worcestershire sauce, flour, salt and pepper.

With floured hands form into 4 cakes.

Heat the oil and butter in a frying pan and fry the cakes over a moderate heat until golden brown on both sides.

Garnish with parsley.

Gwendolen Wilkinson

Babes and Sucklings

The little boy from the city was watching the cows being milked. Then he saw the calves being fed with the milk from the buckets. "I see it all now! They get it when they are little and give it back when they're big!"

Thirza West—Banffshire

Two Ends

Home produce enthusiast talking to another. "My neighbour has suggested that between us we keep a cow. Knowing him I bet he'll keep the end that has to be milked and leave me the end that has to be fed.

Miss B. Herring, Surrey

35

Fritato

1 oz butter
1 tablespoon cooking oil
1 lb potatoes, boiled and sliced ¼ inch
    thick
8 oz courgettes, thinly sliced
8 oz cooked meat, chopped
4 eggs
salt and pepper

Heat the butter and oil in a frying pan and swirl around until the base and sides of the pan are coated.

Place half the potatoes in the pan, followed by the courgettes, the cooked meat and lastly the remaining half of the potatoes.

Whisk the eggs and season with salt and pepper. Pour over the meat and vegetables.

Cover and cook very gently over a low heat, tilting the pan from time to time to allow the egg to run to the sides.

When the egg is almost set place under a medium hot grill to brown the top.

Turn out onto a serving plate and cut into wedges.

Potatoschotel

8 oz onions, sliced
1 tablespoon cooking oil
1 lb potatoes, mashed
12 oz cooked pork, finely chopped
8 oz cooking apples, thinly sliced
¼ teaspoon nutmeg
salt and pepper
¼ pint chicken stock
1 oz white breadcrumbs
1 oz melted butter

Fry the onions in the cooking oil until they are golden brown.

Grease a pie dish and line with ⅔ of the potatoes.

Layer the meat, apples and onions in the bed of potatoes, sprinkle with nutmeg and season with salt and pepper.

Pour the stock over the contents of the dish and then top with the remaining potatoes.

Sprinkle the breadcrumbs over the potatoes and trickle the melted butter over the breadcrumbs.

Cook at 400°F (200°C) Gas Mark 6 for 35 minutes until the topping is crisp and brown.

Taunton Pork Pot

1 tablespoon cooking oil
1 large onion, sliced
4 spare rib chops
1 teaspoon soft brown sugar
salt and pepper
1 oz flour
1 tablespoon tomato purée
1 teaspoon oregano
½ pint dry cider
1 lb potatoes, peeled and thinly sliced
1 oz butter, melted

Heat the cooking oil and fry the onion until golden brown. Remove with a draining spoon to a greased casserole.

Fry the chops on both sides until the meat is sealed. Place in the casserole and sprinkle with the sugar.

Make a paste with the flour and tomato purée then gradually add the cider, salt and pepper and oregano. Pour over the contents of the casserole.

Overlap the potato slices and completely cover the top.

Brush the potatoes with the melted butter and sprinkle with salt.

Cover and cook at 350°F (180°C) Gas Mark 4 for 1 hour. Remove the cover, increase the heat to 400°F (200°C) Gas Mark 6 and cook for a further 20 minutes until the potatoes are crisp and golden brown.

Peasant's Platter

12 oz apples
1 oz sugar
½ oz butter
1½ lb potatoes, mashed
salt and pepper
1 lb black pudding
1 tablespoon cooking oil
2 medium onions, sliced

Peel and core the apples and cook until soft using only sufficient water to prevent them burning. Once they are soft add the sugar and butter and beat until smooth.

Blend the cooked apple into the mashed potato and season with salt and pepper.

Meanwhile heat the cooking oil and fry the slices of black pudding briskly until crisp on both sides. Remove from the pan and fry the onions until golden brown.

Arrange the slices of black pudding round the edge of a serving platter and pile the potato and apple mixture in the centre of the dish.

Scatter the fried onions over the potatoes and serve piping hot.

Liver Fiesta

Serves 4

2 rashers bacon, chopped
1 lb liver, thinly sliced
seasoned flour
1 oz butter
1 large onion, sliced
4 oz tomatoes, skinned and quartered
2 celery sticks, cut into 1 inch pieces
3 tablespoons sherry
¼ pint chicken stock
grated rind of 1 lemon
large pinch nutmeg
salt and pepper
1¼ lb potatoes, parboiled for 10 mins
1 teaspoon cooking oil

Fry the bacon until the fat runs free and remove from the pan.

Dust the liver with seasoned flour. Add the butter to the pan, fry the onion for 3 minutes, then add the liver and brown on both sides.

Add the tomatoes, celery, bacon, sherry, stock, lemon rind, nutmeg and seasoning. Bring to the boil then transfer to a greased casserole.

Cut the potatoes into slices ¼ inch thick and place over the meat. Brush lightly with the oil.

Cover and cook at 350°F (180°C) Gas Mark 4 for 1¼ hours. Remove the lid and cook for a further 15 minutes to crisp and brown the potatoes.

Chicken Ginger Vol-au-Vent

Serves 4

1½ oz butter
1 egg, beaten
1 lb potatoes, cooked and sieved
1 medium onion, chopped
2 oz mushrooms, chopped
½ oz flour
1 rounded teaspoon powdered ginger
½ pint chicken stock
1 rounded teaspoon French mustard
salt and pepper
12 oz cooked chicken, chopped
1 oz flaked almonds

Beat 1 oz of the butter and the egg into the potatoes.

Make a potato vol-au-vent shell by placing the mixture in a piping bag fitted with a No. 10 star nozzle and pipe a 5 inch circular base on a greased ovenproof plate, build up the sides with the remaining potato.

Bake in a hot oven 400°F (200°C) Gas Mark 6 for 15-20 minutes until golden brown.

Melt the remaining ½ oz butter and fry the onion and mushrooms for 5 minutes without colouring the onion. Add the flour and ginger and cook for 1 minute. Gradually stir in the stock and mustard and bring to the boil. Season. Fold in the chicken and simmer for 5 minutes.

Turn this filling into the cooked vol-au-vent case and sprinkle with flaked almonds before serving.

Potato Apfelstrudel

Pastry

4 oz flour
1 teaspoon cooking oil
2 tablespoons warm water
pinch salt

Filling

4 oz apple, finely chopped
4 oz mashed potatoes
2 tablespoons beaten egg
2 oz sugar
2 oz raisins
½ teaspoon cinnamon

To make the strudel pastry sift the flour and salt into a warm bowl. Make a well in the centre and pour in the oil and water. Beat well until the paste is nicely elastic.

Turn onto a pastry board and knead until it becomes smooth and shiny and leaves the hand cleanly.

Put into a clean floured bowl; cover and leave in a warm place for 15 minutes.

Roll on a floured cloth and pull gently from all sides until paper thin. Lay aside for another 15 minutes.

Mix all the filling ingredients together and spread over the pastry.

Roll up like a swiss roll and seal the edge by moistening with water. Transfer carefully to a baking sheet and brush with a little melted butter.

Bake at 400°F (200°C) Gas Mark 6 for 30 minutes.

Serve either hot or cold.

Coffee Dreams

2 oz butter
2 oz castor sugar
3 oz coconut
3 oz rolled oats
2 oz mashed potatoes
2 teaspoons coffee essence
4 oz cooking chocolate

Beat the butter and sugar together until light and creamy.

Fold in the coconut, rolled oats, mashed potatoes and coffee essence and beat until the mixture is well blended.

Roll into 24 little balls, the size of a walnut.

Melt the cooking chocolate in a bowl placed over a pan of hot water and coat each little ball with the chocolate.

Allow to set.

Apricot Delight

1 × 14 oz can apricot halves
2 oz potatoes, boiled
1 oz butter
2 tablespoons milk
3 eggs, separated
2 oz castor sugar
1 teaspoon ground ginger
½ oz flaked almonds

Sieve or liquidise the apricots and pour into the base of a greased 1 ½ -2 pint soufflé dish or casserole.

Mash the potatoes with the butter and milk. Blend in the egg yolks, sugar and ginger.

Whisk the egg whites until stiff and gently fold into the potato mixture. Pour into the dish and top with flaked almonds.

Bake at 350°F (180°C) Gas Mark 4 for 35 minutes until firm, well risen and browned. Serve hot with cream.

Winter

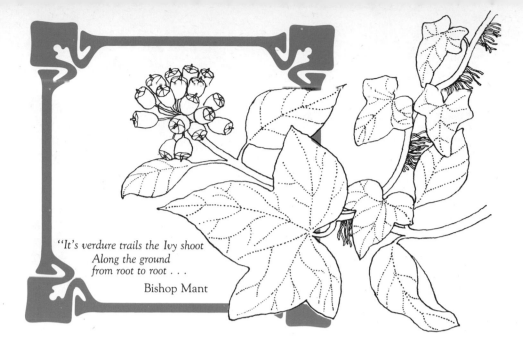

*"It's verdure trails the Ivy shoot
Along the ground
from root to root . . .*

Bishop Mant

Chocolate Potatoes

**6 oz cold potatoes, boiled and
  sieved**
1 oz butter
1 teaspoon vanilla essence
1½ lb icing sugar, sieved
4 oz chocolate vermicelli

Beat the potatoes, butter and flavouring until
smooth.

Gradually fold in the icing sugar until the mixture is
thick enough to knead.

Turn out onto a board and knead until smooth and
satiny.

Roll into small balls each about the size of a walnut
and coat with chocolate vermicelli.

Photo page 40

Parsley and Thyme Pyramids

Serves 4

**2 rounded tablespoons dried parsley
  and thyme stuffing mix**
1½ lb potatoes, boiled and sieved
1 egg, beaten
1 oz butter
grated rind of 1 small lemon
egg/milk glaze

Reconstitute the stuffing mix as directed on the
packet.

Add to the potatoes along with the egg, butter and
lemon rind. Beat well until thoroughly mixed.

Place in a piping bag fitted with a No. 10 star nozzle
and pipe in pyramids on a greased baking sheet.

Brush with egg/milk glaze and cook at 375°F (190°C)
Gas Mark 5 for 20-25 minutes until golden brown.

Photo page 40

Prawn Potato Cocktail

Serves 4

5 tablespoons mayonnaise
2 tablespoons double cream
2 tablespoons tomato purée
1 teaspoon Worcestershire sauce
1 teaspoon lemon juice
1 lb potatoes, cooked and diced
6 oz prawns, shelled
shredded lettuce

Mix together the mayonnaise, double cream, tomato
purée, Worcestershire sauce and lemon juice.

Carefully fold in the potatoes and prawns, reserving a
few prawns for garnishing.

Allow to stand for at least 1 hour to bring out the full
flavour.

Serve on a bed of shredded lettuce and garnish with
the reserved prawns.

Photo page 40

Picture shows: Chocolate Potatoes, Prawn Potato Cocktail, Candied Cheesecake *(page 42)*,
Californian Duck *(page 42)*, Parsley and Thyme Pyramids.

Candied Cheesecake

Serves 4

6 oz shortcrust pastry
2 oz butter
4 oz potatoes, mashed
2 oz caster sugar
2 oz candied peel
3 tablespoons cream
2 eggs
marzipan fruits to decorate

Line a 6 inch flan tin with the pastry and bake blind for 15 minutes at 400°F (200°C) Gas Mark 6.

Beat the butter into the potatoes then mix in the sugar, candied peel and cream. Stir in 1 whole egg and 1 egg yolk.

Whisk the remaining egg white until stiff, then gently fold into the mixture.

Turn into the pastry case and bake at 350°F (180°C) Gas Mark 4 for 50 minutes.

Decorate with marzipan fruits.   *Photo page 40*

Californian Duck

Serves 4

1 × 5 lb duck

Stuffing

1 medium onion, chopped
2 celery sticks, chopped
½ oz butter
8 oz sausagemeat
2 egg yolks
1 lb potatoes, mashed
2 oz walnuts, chopped
1 × 15 oz can apricots,
  drained and sliced
salt and pepper

Prepare the stuffing by frying the onion and celery in the butter until the onion is soft but not coloured.

Beat the sausagemeat, egg yolks and potatoes together until well blended.

Fold in the onion, celery, walnuts and apricots. Season.

Stuff the duck and secure firmly with wooden cocktail sticks.

Place the duck in a roasting tin. Cover with aluminium foil and cook at 375°F (190°C) Gas Mark 5 for 2-2½ hours until cooked and golden brown. Remove the aluminium foil for the last 30 minutes of cooking time to allow the bird to brown. Remove the cocktail sticks.

Serve with roast potatoes, parsley and thyme pyramids and green peas.

Cheese Prawn Bakes

Serves 4

4 × 8 oz ready baked potatoes
1 oz butter
2 oz cheese spread
1 × 3¼ oz tin prawns
salt and pepper
1 tablespoon parsley, chopped

Remove a slice from the top of the potatoes, and scoop the flesh into a bowl.

Mash the potatoes with the butter and cheese spread and fold in the prawns. Season.

Pile the mixture back into the potato skins and reheat in a hot oven.

Garnish with the chopped parsley.

Twelfth Night Soup

Serves 4

1 large onion, sliced
1 oz butter
6 oz cooked chicken or turkey
  scraps
4 oz left over stuffing
8 oz potatoes, mashed
1 × 15 oz tin tomatoes
1 × 8 oz tin carrots, sliced
1 tablespoon tomato purée
2 pints stock
salt and pepper

Lightly fry the onion in the butter.

Add all the other ingredients to the pan, seasoning to taste. Stir well.

Bring to the boil and simmer for 15 minutes.

This soup can be sieved or liquidised but is much better served as a thick chunky soup; a meal in itself.

Shepherdess Pie

Serves 4

1 lb minced beef
1 medium onion, sliced
1 × 8 oz tin tomatoes
1 beef stock cube
½ teaspoon crushed rosemary
salt and pepper
8 oz potatoes, boiled
8 oz carrots, cooked
freshly ground black pepper

Fry the mince and onion briskly for 5 minutes. Pour off any excess fat from the mince.

Add the tin of tomatoes, stock cube, rosemary and seasoning. Cover and simmer for 20 minutes.

Mash the potatoes and carrots together. Season well with black pepper.

Place the meat mixture in a pie dish and cover with the potatoes and carrots. Fork the top to give a thatched effect.

Cook at 350°F (180°C) Gas Mark 4 for 30 minutes.

Photo page 2

Treacle Pudding

Serves 4

8 oz potatoes, boiled and sieved
4 oz self raising flour
2 oz white breadcrumbs
3 oz shredded suet
4 oz sultanas
3 tablespoons black treacle
2 oz caster sugar
1 tablespoon milk

Mix all the ingredients together very thoroughly.

Turn into a greased pudding basin.

Cover with greaseproof paper. Tie a pudding cloth or aluminium foil over the paper and steam the pudding for 2 hours.

Serve hot with whipped cream or custard as an accompaniment.

Photo page 2

About *The Countryman*

FOR fifty-two years the familiar little green magazine has been coming from the Oxfordshire countryside, concerning itself with rural problems and delighting thousands of devoted readers who never throw a copy away. It is sharp, outspoken and concerned with the problems of the day; it is also amusing and maintains high standards in its writing, drawings and photographs. It is read with respect by the

powerful in Whitehall and enjoyed by the cottagers. It has, too, a large urban readership among people who would be countrymen if they could, or who take their recreation there, and one of its functions is to make the two sides of the nation understand the needs and problems of each other. For many thousands overseas it comes as a breath of fresh native air.

Though it pays proper respect to the days gone by, and disappearing crafts and customs, it will never indulge in nostalgia or whimsy. It is concerned with reality, and whatever its subjects the author can be accepted as an authority, probably the best in his field. Princes and Prime Ministers write for it, poachers and judges, lorry drivers and university dons, great naturalists and simple gardeners.

It is edited from Sheep Street, Burford, Oxford, is published quarterly and can be obtained from newsagents, price 60p or by annual subscription from the Circulation Department, The Countryman, Watling Street, Milton Keynes, for £3 a year.

Bedfordshire County Pie

Serves 8

Pastry

4 oz lard or white fat
¼ pint milk
10 oz plain flour
½ teaspoon salt

Filling

**1 lb potatoes, peeled and sliced
  ¼ inch thick**
12 oz carrots, thinly sliced
12 oz onions, roughly chopped
8 oz white Cheddar cheese, grated
2 eggs, beaten
¼ pint milk
salt and pepper

Make the pastry by putting the lard and milk into a saucepan and heating until the fat melts.

Stir in the flour and salt and keep beating until a soft paste is formed. Lay aside for 10 minutes to cool and firm slightly.

Meanwhile boil the potatoes, carrots and onions in salted water for 5 minutes. Drain.

Take a 6 ½ inch loose bottomed cake tin and line it with ¾ of the pastry, kneading it into place with fingers if necessary.

Layer the partly cooked vegetables and the cheese in the pastry shell.

Blend the eggs and milk together, season and pour over the vegetables and cheese. Reserve one tablespoon of the liquid to glaze the top of the pie.

Roll out the remaining pastry to form a lid for the pie. Brush the edges of the pastry shell with water. Place the lid on top and seal the edges with finger and thumb.

Make a slit in the centre to allow steam to escape and brush the top with the leftover egg and milk.

Bake at 400°F (200°C) Gas Mark 6 for 30 minutes then reduce the heat to 350°F (180°C) Gas Mark 4 for a further 30 minutes.

This pie can be eaten either hot or cold.

Split Green Pea and Potato Soup

Serves 4

**8 oz potatoes, peeled and cut into
  chunks**
**8 oz split green peas, soaked
  overnight**
2 celery sticks, roughly chopped
1 oz butter
1½ pints chicken stock
salt and pepper
½ pint milk
**2 oz streaky bacon, very crisply
  grilled and crushed**

Toss the potatoes, split green peas and celery in the melted butter for 2-3 minutes over a gentle heat.

Add the stock and seasoning and simmer for 1-1 ½ hours.

Sieve or liquidise the soup. Return to the pan and add the milk and bacon.

Check the seasoning and bring back to the boil before serving.

Cream of Potato and Carrot Soup

Serves 4

2 oz butter
2 onions sliced
2 cloves garlic, crushed
1½ lb carrots, sliced
1 lb potatoes, peeled and sliced
2 pints chicken stock
salt and pepper
1 teaspoon dried basil
toast croûtons to garnish

Melt the butter and fry the onion and garlic for 5 minutes.

Add the carrots, potatoes, stock, seasoning and basil.

Bring to the boil and simmer for 1 hour.

Sieve or liquidise the soup. Check the seasoning and reheat.

Garnish with the toast croûtons.

Quick Potato and Leek Soup

Serves 4

2 medium leeks, chopped
1 medium onion, finely chopped
1 oz butter
8 oz potatoes, mashed
1½ -2 pints chicken stock using
   2 stock cubes
salt and pepper
4 tablespoons single cream
1 tablespoon parsley, chopped

Fry the leeks and onion in the butter until soft but not coloured.

Whisk the mashed potatoes into the chicken stock, the less stock the thicker the soup. Add the leeks and onion. Season.

Bring to the boil and simmer for 15 minutes.

Pour into individual bowls; swirl with cream and garnish with parsley.

Tattie Drottle

Serves 4

1½ lb potatoes, peeled and
   quartered
1 lb swede turnip, cut into 1 inch
   cubes
8 oz carrots, sliced
1 large onion, chopped
2 pints white stock
salt and pepper
1 pint milk
1 tablespoon parsley, chopped

Put all the prepared vegetables into a large pan with the stock and seasoning.

Bring to the boil and simmer for 1 hour.

Sieve or liquidise the soup. Return to the pan, add the milk and bring back to boiling point.

Adjust the seasoning if necessary and serve garnished with chopped parsley.

Potato Mulligatawny Soup

Serves 6

8 oz onions, chopped
2 oz butter
1 level dessertspoon curry powder
1 lb potatoes, peeled and cut into
   chunks
8 oz carrots, sliced
1 cooking apple, peeled and
   chopped
2½ pints beef stock
salt and pepper
½ pint milk
squeeze of lemon juice

Fry the onions in the butter until slightly coloured. Add the curry powder and fry for 2-3 minutes.

Add the potatoes, carrots, apple and stock. Season and simmer for 50 minutes.

Sieve or liquidise. Return to the pan with the milk and lemon juice. Reheat before serving.

Grading Potatoes

Before potatoes are sent to the markets and shops they have to be graded. The diseased, damaged and greened potatoes, also the very small and very large ones, must be removed and no potatoes should be sold which do not comply with a standard set by the Potato Marketing Board. Every bag has to be marked not only with the name of the variety of potatoes it contains but also bear a name or number whereby sub-standard potatoes can be traced back to their source of origin. The Board has a team of Market Inspectors who visit farms, markets and shops and who help to enforce quality standards.

Jacket Potato Supper

Serves 4

4 × 8 oz ready baked potatoes
salt and pepper
1 tablespoon milk
1 small onion, finely chopped
1 oz butter
4 tomatoes, skinned and chopped
4 oz lean bacon, chopped
1 tablespoon Worcestershire sauce
1 oz Cheshire cheese, grated

Cut a slice from the top of the potatoes. Scoop the flesh into a bowl and mash with the salt, pepper and milk.

Fry the onion in the butter until soft then stir in the tomatoes, bacon and Worcestershire sauce. Season. Simmer for 5 minutes.

Blend together the potatoes and the ham mixture and pile back into the potato skins.

Wrap in foil leaving the tops open.

Sprinkle with cheese and reheat in a hot oven.

Farmhouse Bakes

Serves 4

4 × 8 oz ready baked potatoes
1 oz butter
1 teaspoon made mustard
salt and pepper
4 lamb's kidneys, skinned, cored
    and grilled
4 rashers streaky bacon, crisply
    grilled

Remove a slice from the top of the potatoes.

Scoop the flesh into a bowl. Beat in the butter and mustard, season with salt and pepper.

Chop the kidneys and bacon and add to the potatoes.

Pile the mixture back into the potato skins and reheat in a hot oven.

Chestnut Balls

Serves 4

6 oz potatoes, mashed
4 oz chestnut purée, unsweetened
pinch dry mustard
1 egg, beaten
salt and pepper

Coating

1 oz flour
1 egg beaten
12 cream crackers, crushed
deep fat for frying

Blend the potatoes, chestnut purée, mustard and egg together. Season well and chill for 1 hour.

Shape into balls the size of a golf ball. Roll in the flour, the beaten egg and lastly the cracker crumbs.

Fry in deep fat until crisp and golden. Drain on kitchen paper.

Pommes Dauphinoise

Serves 4

1 lb potatoes, peeled and thinly
    sliced
4 oz Cheddar cheese, grated
salt and pepper
½ pint milk
2 eggs
1 clove garlic, crushed
pinch of nutmeg
1 oz butter

Layer the potatoes and cheese in a fairly shallow ovenproof dish. Season with salt and pepper.

Beat the milk, eggs, garlic and nutmeg together and pour over the potatoes and cheese. Dot with the butter.

Bake at 375°F (190°C) Gas Mark 5 for 40 minutes.

Pommes Berrichone

Serves 4

1¼ lb potatoes, peeled and diced
¼ lb bacon, cut into snippets
¼ lb onions, finely chopped
1 tablespoon parsley, chopped
salt and pepper
¼ pint beef stock
1 oz butter, melted

Mix the potatoes, bacon, onions and parsley together in a casserole. Season with salt and pepper.

Pour the stock over the contents of the casserole and brush the top with melted butter.

Cook at 400°F (200°C) Gas Mark 6 for 40-45 minutes until the potatoes are cooked and the top is crusty and brown.

Minced Beef and Potato Pudding

Serves 4

Suet Paste

8 oz S.R. flour
½ teaspoon salt
½ teaspoon baking powder
2 oz shredded suet
2 oz potatoes, peeled and grated
water to bind

Filling

12 oz minced beef
1 medium onion, chopped
6 oz potatoes, peeled and diced
1 medium green pepper, finely
    chopped
2 tablespoons tomato purée
¼ pint beef stock
salt and pepper

Sieve the flour, salt and baking powder into a bowl. Add the suet and the grated potatoes. Blend to a soft dough with water.

Lay aside ⅓ of the paste. Line a greased 2 pint pudding basin with the remainder of the paste.

Fry the mince briskly without any fat until browned. Add the onions, potato and green pepper and cook gently for a further 5 minutes.

Pour in the tomato purée and stock. Season with salt and pepper and bring to the boil. Turn into the pastry lined basin.

Roll out the remaining paste and cover the top of the pudding. Seal the edges with water.

Cover securely with greased foil. Place in a pan of boiling water and steam for 1½ hours.

Wheelwright

When Frank was young and huge as a Clydesdale,
He chose the timber for his cart,
Measured the wood and seasoned it,
Then scraped each interlocking part.—

Those two great wheels to take the load-weight,
And every axle, shaft and spoke:
Elm for the massive planks and stocks,
The starring wheel-spokes turned from oak.

He built it well. For forty years
His wagon carried muck to spread,
Swung with its towering load of hay
And hauled the harvest to the shed.

Then tractors shouldered it aside,
Hub-deep in nettle, vetch and gorse,
It shares this corner of the farm
With horse-plough and a pensioned horse.

And here it stands, all life behind,
Drag-shoe and drip-chain long since gone.
Some spokes are gaps, like missing teeth,
The floor-planks worn by rain and sun.

While Frank, forgotten in his ward,
With dwindled frame and silent tongue,
Remembers in dim happiness
When wheelwright, wheels and world were young.

Clive Sansom

Potato and Egg Curry

6 oz onions, chopped
3 oz butter
1½ oz flour
1 oz mild curry powder
1 oz tomato purée
2 oz apple chopped
1 pint stock
2 oz sultanas
juice and rind of ½ lemon
2 tablespoons redcurrant jelly
salt and pepper
1 lb potatoes, boiled and cut into
    large dice
4 eggs hardboiled and halved
    lengthwise
1 tablespoon parsley, chopped

Fry the onion in the melted butter until slightly brown.

Add the flour, curry powder, tomato purée and apple and continue to cook for another five minutes.

Pour in the stock gradually and bring to the boil.

Add the sultanas, lemon juice, rind and redcurrant jelly. Season.

Toss the potatoes and hardboiled eggs in the curry sauce and simmer for about 5 minutes.

Serve very hot, garnished with chopped parsley.

Welsh Supper

2 medium leeks, trimmed and cut
    into 1 inch lengths
1 oz butter
1 oz flour
½ pint milk
salt and pepper
5 oz cheese, grated
4 eggs, hard boiled and sliced
1 lb potatoes, cooked and cut into
    slices ¼ inch thick

Cook the leeks in boiling salted water for 5 minutes. Drain.

Melt the butter in a saucepan, stir in the flour and cook for 1-2 minutes without browning. Gradually pour in the milk, beating well as you do so.

Bring the sauce to the boil. Season. Remove the pan from the heat and stir in 3 oz of the cheese.

Place a layer of egg slices in the bottom of a greased pie dish; follow this with a layer of leeks then a layer of potatoes. Repeat the layers once more.

Pour the cheese sauce over the eggs and vegetables and scatter the remaining cheese on top.

Cook at 400°F (200°C) Gas Mark 6 for 40 minutes until golden brown.

Shepherd's Delight

1 tablespoon cooking oil
1 lb lean cut lamb, coarsely minced
salt and pepper
8 oz cabbage, chopped
½ pint pouring onion sauce
1 lb potatoes, boiled and sieved
1 oz butter
1 egg, beaten

Heat the oil and gently fry the minced lamb for 10 minutes. Season with salt and pepper.

Meanwhile plunge the cabbage into boiling salted water and cook rapidly for 10 minutes.

Drain the cabbage and place in a greased casserole in alternating layers with the lamb.

Prepare the onion sauce and pour over the contents of the casserole.

Beat the potatoes with the butter and egg until really smooth.

Place in a piping bag fitted with a No. 10 star nozzle and pipe over the top of the casserole.

Cook at 375°F (190°C) Gas Mark 5 for 30 minutes until the potatoes are browned.

Beef Crock-pot

1 lb stewing steak, cut into pieces
1 oz seasoned flour
1 tablespoon cooking oil
4 oz prunes, soaked
½ teaspoon mixed herbs
2 tablespoons chutney
½ pint beef stock
¼ pint Guinness
salt and pepper
1 lb potatoes, peeled and thinly
   sliced
1 oz butter, melted

Toss the steak in the seasoned flour.

Heat the oil in a frying pan and brown the meat on all sides.

Add the prunes, herbs, chutney, stock, Guinness, salt and pepper and bring to the boil.

Turn into a greased casserole. Top with overlapping slices of potato and brush them with a little melted butter.

Cover with a lid or foil and cook at 325°F (170°C) Gas Mark 3 for 2 hours. Uncover and increase the heat to 400°F (200°C) Gas Mark 6 for a further 30 minutes to brown the potatoes.

Spiced Potato and Cucumber

Serves 4

1 lb potatoes, diced
8 oz cucumber, cut into 1 inch
   cubes
1 oz butter
1 oz flour
½ pint milk
¼ teaspoon crushed cumin seed
large pinch cayenne pepper
salt
3 eggs, hard boiled and
   roughly chopped
4 oz Lancashire cheese, grated

Boil the potatoes and cucumber in salted water for approximately 5 minutes until just tender. Drain.

Make a sauce by melting the butter stirring in the flour and cooking for 1-2 minutes. Gradually pour in the milk stirring constantly. Season with the cumin, cayenne and salt.

Toss the potatoes, cucumber and hard boiled eggs in the sauce and simmer for 5 minutes.

Turn into a greased heatproof dish. Sprinkle with the cheese and flash under a hot grill until bubbly brown.

Cinderella Pie

Serves 4

1 lb potatoes, boiled and cut into
   slices ¼ inch thick
2 eggs, hard boiled and sliced
½ oz butter
½ oz flour
½ pint milk
1 tablespoon anchovy essence
salt and pepper
4 oz Cheshire cheese, grated

Place the potatoes in a greased casserole and cover with the sliced hard boiled eggs.

Melt the butter and stir in the flour, cook for 1-2 minutes without browning. Gradually add the milk, stirring constantly. Add the anchovy essence, salt and pepper.

Pour the sauce over the eggs and sprinkle with the cheese.

Cook at 450°F (230°C) Gas Mark 8 for 15-20 minutes.

Newfoundland Plate Pie

Serves 4

1 lb potatoes, mashed
1 small teaspoon made mustard
1 egg yolk
1 × 6 oz packet frozen 'Cod in
   Shrimp Sauce'
4 tomatoes, peeled and sliced
2 oz Cheddar cheese, grated

Blend together the potatoes, mustard and egg yolk and spread over a greased ovenproof plate.

Cook at 400°F (200°C) Gas Mark 6 for 10 minutes.

Meanwhile cook the fish as directed on the packet. Flake the fish and mix through the shrimp sauce.

Spread over the potato base. Cover with sliced tomatoes and sprinkle with cheese.

Cook at 400°F (200°C) Gas Mark 6 for a further 10 minutes.

Potato and Vegetable Broth

Serves 4

2 oz onion, chopped
2 oz leek, chopped
2 oz celery, diced
2 oz butter
2 oz tomatoes, skinned and
    chopped
8 oz potatoes, peeled and diced
1 oz cabbage, shredded
2 pints stock
salt and pepper
bouquet garni, optional

Sauté the onion, leek and celery in the butter until soft but not coloured.

Add all the other vegetables, stock, seasoning and bouquet garni.

Bring to the boil and simmer for 40 minutes until the vegetables are tender.

Remove the bouquet garni and adjust the seasoning before serving.

Photo page 51

Baker's Porkpot

Serves 4

1¼ lb shoulder of pork, cut into
    1 inch cubes
8 oz large pork sausages
1 onion, chopped
3 carrots, sliced
3 celery sticks, chopped
1 level tablespoon flour
1 pint chicken stock
½ level teaspoon dried rosemary
1 teaspoon soy sauce
salt and pepper
1 lb potatoes, parboiled and sliced
2 teaspoons French mustard

Fry the pork and sausages gently in their own fat until the sausages are lightly browned.

Remove the pork and sausages to a deep casserole dish.

Fry the onion, carrots and celery for 5 minutes in the pork fat.

Stir in the flour and rosemary and blend in the stock and soy sauce. Season. Bring to the boil, then pour over the meat in the casserole.

Cover and cook at 350°F (180°C) Gas Mark 4 for 45 minutes. Remove from the oven.

Spread the potato slices liberally with French mustard and place on the casserole, mustard side uppermost.

Return the dish to the oven and cook for a further 45 minutes.

Serve piping hot.

Photo page 51

Trawler Pie

Serves 4

1 lb white fish cut into 1 inch cubes
4 oz mushrooms, sliced
2 tomatoes, skinned and sliced
salt and pepper
¼ pint cider
¾ oz butter
¾ oz flour
1 lb potatoes, mashed
2 oz cheese, finely grated

Arrange the fish, mushrooms and tomatoes in a shallow casserole, with seasoning to taste. Add the cider.

Cover and cook for 30 minutes at 375°F (190°C) Gas Mark 5. Strain off the liquor.

Melt the butter in a saucepan and stir in the flour, gradually add the fish liquor beating well. Bring to the boil and simmer for 2 minutes. Season.

Pour the sauce over the contents of the casserole.

Fold the grated cheese into the hot mashed potatoes and beat until the cheese has melted. Place in a piping bag and with a No. 10 star nozzle pipe the potatoes over the fish.

Return to the oven and increase the heat to 425°F (220°C) Gas Mark 7 for 15 minutes until the topping has browned.

Picture shows: Potato and Vegetable Broth, Bakers Porkpot, Turkey Coronet, *(page 53)*, Sweet and Sour Bacon *(page 52)*. ▶

Sweet and Sour Bacon

12 oz lean bacon, cut into strips
1 onion, chopped
1 oz butter
1 oz flour
¾ pint white stock
**1½ lb potatoes, cooked and sliced
¼ inch thick**
**1 × 8 oz pack frozen green beans,
sliced**
1 tablespoon wine vinegar
1 teaspoon sugar
salt and pepper

Gently fry the bacon and onion in the butter for 5 minutes.

Stir in the flour and cook gently for 2-3 minutes. Gradually add the stock and bring to the boil stirring continuously.

To this sauce add the potatoes, beans, wine vinegar, sugar, salt and pepper to taste.

Cover and simmer gently for 30 minutes. Serve piping hot.

Photo page 51

Weather outlook

Beyond the winter-darkened copse,
Etched razor-sharp upon the sky-line,
A sea of red and gold,
Dusking to pearly grey.
Smoke from cottage chimneys
Bends to the east.
Seven days of bitter frost.
There should be snow by morning.

R. R. Zanber

A snowy lane in the Avon Valley
Photo: John S. Beswick

Dickory Dock

I HAD been troubled with mice in the kitchen; and though I tried all types of trap, keeping a cat and filling up holes as fast as they were made, the mice always came back. One night, disturbed by their scrabblings but still half asleep, I suddenly thought I would get the alarm clock—one of the old-fashioned sort—and put it on the kitchen floor. Its loud tick reverberated through the boards, and in the morning there was no sign of a mouse. The following night I rewound the clock and put it back on the floor, with a second one alongside and some tempting cake; this remained untouched. I now keep both clocks on the floor, ticking merrily, and have not seen another mouse.

A. B. Quine

Beetroot Delight

Serves 4

2 oz butter
1 large onion, chopped
1 lb beetroot, uncooked and grated
1 large cooking apple, grated
12 oz potatoes, peeled and diced
salt and pepper
3 tablespoons vinegar
1 teaspoon sugar

Melt the butter in a frying pan and fry the onion gently.

Add the beetroot, apple and the potatoes and toss them in the butter. Season, then pour in the vinegar and sugar.

Cover the pan and cook gently until the mixture is soft. Shake the pan occasionally to prevent the contents sticking.

This dish is delicious served with thick grilled sausages.

Leek Flan

Serves 4

Pastry

3 oz butter
4 oz flour
4 oz potatoes, boiled and sieved
1 teaspoon baking powder
¼ teaspoon salt

Filling

8 oz leeks, cut into 1 inch lengths
1 oz butter
2 eggs, beaten
¼ pint single cream
salt and black pepper

Rub the fat into the flour; add the potatoes, baking powder and salt and knead to a smooth dough.

Line a 7 inch flan tin with the pastry. Bake blind at 400°F (200°C) Gas Mark 6 for 10 minutes. Remove from the oven.

Sauté the leeks in the butter for approximately 5 minutes without letting them colour, then spread them over the base of the flan case.

Beat the eggs, cream and seasoning together and pour over the leeks.

Reduce the oven heat to 350°F (180°C) Gas Mark 4 and cook for 25 minutes until the flan filling has set.

Turkey Coronet

Serves 4

2 eggs, beaten
1½ oz butter
2 lbs potatoes, mashed
1 small onion finely chopped
½ oz flour
½ pint white wine
1 level teaspoon rosemary
2 teaspoons Worcestershire sauce
2 level teaspoons paprika pepper
1 lb cooked turkey, diced
salt and pepper
watercress for garnishing

Beat the eggs, reserving a little for glazing, and 1 oz of the butter into the potatoes.

Grease a 6 inch loose bottomed cake tin and line the tin with the potatoes. Brush the inside of the potato shell with the reserved beaten egg.

Cook at 400°F (200°C) Gas Mark 6 for 30 minutes until lightly browned.

Remove carefully from the tin, place on an ovenproof serving dish and keep warm.

Make the filling by melting the remaining ½ oz butter and frying the onion until soft and transparent. Stir in the flour and cook for 1-2 minutes. Gradually pour in the wine, stirring as you do so.

Add the rosemary, Worcestershire sauce, paprika pepper and turkey dice. Season.

Pour into the potato shell and garnish with watercress.

Photo page 51

Cheddar Fish

1½ lb potatoes, boiled
1 oz butter
1 egg, beaten
1 lb white fish
½ pint milk
½ oz butter
½ oz flour
2 oz Cheddar cheese, grated
1 tablespoon chutney
salt and pepper
1 oz soft white breadcrumbs

Mash the potatoes thoroughly with the butter and egg.

Place the potato mixture in a piping bag fitted with a No. 10 star nozzle and pipe a double ring of duchesse potato round the edge of a pie plate.

Poach the fish in the milk for 5 minutes. Strain off the milk, reserving same and flake the fish into the centre of the plate.

Melt the butter in a saucepan, stir in the flour then gradually add the milk in which the fish was poached, stirring as you do so. Bring to the boil.

Remove from the heat and stir in the cheese and chutney. Season to taste.

Pour the sauce over the fish and sprinkle the top with breadcrumbs.

Flash under a hot grill until the top is golden brown.

Smoked Haddock Bake

12 oz smoked haddock
1½ lb potatoes, parboiled and
    sliced
salt and pepper
2 onions, thinly sliced
¾ pint milk
2 large eggs, beaten
1 oz butter

Skin the fish if necessary and cut into bite sized pieces.

Place a layer of potatoes in the bottom of a greased 2 pint pie dish. Season well then add a layer of fish and onion.

Repeat once more and finish with a layer of potatoes.

Mix the milk and eggs together and pour over the contents of the pie dish.

Dot with butter and cook at 375°F (190°C) Gas Mark 5 for 50 minutes.

Marinaded Steak Pot

1½ lb chuck steak
1 lb potatoes, peeled and cut into
    chunks
3 tablespoons garlic vinegar
1 tablespoon cooking oil
1½ oz flour
4 oz button onions
4 oz mushrooms
4 rashers streaky bacon, derinded
    and chopped
1 pint beef stock
salt and pepper
1 level tablespoon tomato purée
bouquet garni

Cut the meat into cubes and place in a polythene bag with the potatoes and vinegar. Secure the top and marinade overnight.

Drain and reserve the liquor. Toss the meat in the flour and fry briskly in the oil until browned. Place in a casserole.

Reduce the heat and fry the onions, mushrooms and bacon for 5 minutes.

Add to the casserole with the reserved liquor, stock, salt and pepper, tomato purée and bouquet garni.

Cover and cook at 325°F (170°C) Gas Mark 3 for 1½ hours.

Adjust the seasoning and remove the bouquet garni before serving.

Spicy Pot Roast

Serves 8

1 tablespoon cooking oil
2-2½ lb fresh silverside
2 cloves garlic, crushed
1 onion, sliced
2 teaspoons dried basil
2 teaspoons made mustard
½ teaspoon ground allspice
1 tablespoon soy sauce
2 tablespoons honey
1 × 15 oz can tomatoes
salt and pepper
1½ lb potatoes, peeled and cut into chunks
2 large carrots, scraped and sliced

Heat the cooking oil in a large pan and brown the meat on all sides. Transfer to a large casserole.

To the pan juices add the garlic, onion, basil, mustard, allspice, soy sauce, honey, tomatoes, salt and pepper, and cook gently for 2-3 minutes.

Pour the mixture over the meat. Cover and cook at 350°F (180°C) Gas Mark 4 for 1-1½ hours.

Add the potatoes and carrots and continue cooking for a further 1 hour.

Place the meat in the centre of a serving dish and surround with the vegetables and gravy.

Clapshot

Serves 4

1½ lb potatoes, peeled and quartered
1½ lb swede turnips, cubed
2 oz butter
2 teaspoons dried chives
salt and black pepper

Prepare the potatoes and turnip and boil them in the usual way until they are tender.

Drain and mash together until well blended.

Beat in the butter, chives and seasoning.

Serve piping hot.

A shepherd's version of the 23rd psalm

THUR LORD is me shepherd, I sharn' want fer nothin'.
He goes afore me over thur green dowans, an' guides me
    by thur quiet waters o' thur Adur.
He comforts me soul, an' leads me along goods paaths fer
    His naame's sake.
Yea, though I walks through thur shadowery ways I aunt
    afeared, for His shepherd's crook'll guide.
He'll fin' a quiet plaace fer to eat ower food arter we
    overcome ower difficulties an' us'll be haappy.
Shurly this loveliness 'ul be wi' me aul me days till I
    coome to thur hoome of me Lord fer ever.

In June 1946 an old shepherd recited this to me, surrounded by his flock, on the downs above Steyning in Sussex.—Kathleen Lee

The River Adur near Dial Post
Photo by Kenneth Scowen

Stovies

Serves 4

2 oz beef dripping
2 large onions, sliced
2 lb potatoes, peeled and cut into
   1 inch cubes
salt and pepper
½ pint water

Melt the dripping and fry the onions in a heavy bottomed saucepan until well browned.

Add the potatoes sprinkling them well with salt and pepper. Pour the water over the vegetables.

Cover tightly and cook gently for 45 minutes, shaking the pan occasionally. Just before serving give the pan a good shake.

To make tasty stovies you need good floury potatoes.

Originally stovies were served as a meal on their own. Nowadays some people add cooked meat or sausages to the dish but this is not traditional.

Beef Dolmades

Serves 4

1 small cabbage
1 large onion, chopped
1 oz butter
4 oz mushrooms, sliced
salt and pepper
1 level teaspoon mixed herbs
2 dessertspoons tomato purée
1 lb cooked beef, finely minced
12 oz potatoes, mashed
2 oz flour
1 pint beef stock

Separate the cabbage leaves and plunge them into boiling salted water for 3-4 minutes until they are pliable. Drain.

Prepare the stuffing by gently frying the onion in the butter until transparent, add the mushrooms and fry for a further few minutes. Stir in the salt and pepper, mixed herbs and tomato purée.

Blend the minced meat, the potatoes and the contents of the frying pan together.

Place one tablespoonful of the stuffing on each cabbage leaf and fold them into small parcels. Secure with wooden cocktail sticks.

Coat each parcel with flour and pack them tightly into a fairly shallow casserole dish. Pour the stock over the parcels.

Cover and cook at 350°F (180°C) Gas Mark 4 for 45 minutes. Remove the cocktail sticks.

Serve with plain fluffy jacket baked potatoes.

King Edward's Crown Roast

Serves 4

1 prepared crown roast of lamb
1 oz butter, melted

Nutty Forcemeat

1 small onion, chopped
2 celery sticks, chopped
4 oz mushrooms, sliced
2 oz butter
1 lb potatoes, mashed
4 oz walnuts, chopped
2 tablespoons parsley, chopped
1 egg, beaten
salt and pepper

Fry the onion, celery and mushrooms in the butter until the onion is transparent.

Fold the fried vegetables into the potatoes along with the walnuts, parsley and beaten egg. Season.

Place the crown of lamb in a roasting tin and pack the forcemeat into the centre of the roast.

Brush the crown with melted butter and cover the tips of the bones with aluminium foil.

Cook at 400°F (200°C) Gas Mark 6 for 10 minutes. Reduce the heat to 350°F (180°C) Gas Mark 4 and continue cooking for a further 1 hour.

Remove the aluminium foil and decorate the tips of the bones with cutlet frills.

Serve with roast potatoes and green peas.

Bacon and Bean Pot

Serves 4

8 oz bacon, derinded and diced
8 oz potatoes, peeled and cut into
   large dice
8 oz haricot beans, soaked overnight
1 large parsnip, diced
2 carrots, diced
2 onions, sliced
salt and pepper
2 tablespoons Worcestershire sauce
¾ pint tomato juice

Scone Topping

6 oz flour
½ teaspoon baking powder
½ teaspoon salt
1 oz butter
4 oz potatoes, mashed
5-6 tablespoons milk

Fry the bacon briskly in its own fat. Place in a casserole with the potatoes, haricot beans, parsnip, carrots, onions, salt and pepper.

Mix the Worcestershire sauce with the tomato juice and pour into the casserole.

Cover and cook at 350°F (180°C) Gas Mark 4 for 1¼-1½ hours. Remove from the oven and increase the temperature to 450°F (230°C) Gas Mark 8.

Make the scone topping by sieving together the flour, baking powder and salt. Rub in the butter. Blend in the potatoes and add sufficient milk to give a soft dough.

Roll out on a floured board to form a circle large enough to cover the casserole. Place over the bacon and bean mixture.

Brush with a little milk and return to the oven for 15-20 minutes until well risen and golden brown.

Winter night

Night comes farming the skies, liming with
moonlight
The dark acres, and broadcasts a crop
Of stars then calls up wind to shepherd
Clouds away; I watch their packed fleeces move
Slowly across the hill. Clear for the
Harrow of frost lies the ploughed valley.

Teresa L. Gray

Traces

HERE beneath the hazel boughs
Lie broken scraps of shell,
To mark where, in October days,
The squirrel feasted well.

A five-toed track across the shore,
A scale upon the sand;
Here the otter swam last night
And brought his kill to land.

Errant feathers on the grass
Like opals thrown away;
The sparrowhawk was hunting here
And feathers decked his prey.

Ice-cream cups and paper bags,
The signs are plain to read.
No woodcraft needed here to say
What creature paused to feed.

Gavin A. MacLaren

Fox

Country Code

The Country Code is an excellent document but it is not so easily remembered as the American version—

    Take nothing but pictures
    Leave nothing but footprints
    Kill nothing but time.

Potato Cheese Scones

8 oz potatoes, mashed
2 oz flour
2 oz cheese, grated
¼ teaspoon salt

Place all the ingredients in a bowl and blend together until a paste is formed.
On a floured board roll out to about ⅛ inch thick.
With a 2½ inch scone cutter cut into rounds.
Fry quickly in a greased frying pan or griddle until browned on both sides. Cool in a folded napkin.
Serve spread with butter.

Apple and Prune Hotpot

Serves 4

1½ lb shoulder pork, cut into 1 inch cubes
1 oz seasoned flour
1 oz butter
2 medium onions, sliced
1 lb potatoes, peeled and cut into chunks
1 large apple, peeled and sliced
4 oz prunes, soaked
1 teaspoon made mustard
½ pint white stock
salt and pepper

Toss the pork in the seasoned flour.
Melt the butter and gently fry the onions until soft. Remove from the pan.
Increase the heat and brown the cubes of pork on all sides.
Turn the pork, onions, potatoes, apple and prunes into a casserole making sure everything is well mixed.
Blend the mustard with the stock and seasoning and pour over the contents of the casserole.
Cover and cook at 325°F (170°C) Gas Mark 3 for 2 hours.

Porker's Layer

Serves 4

1 lb potatoes, peeled and cut into chunks
1 lb lean boneless pork, cut into 1 inch pieces
8 oz onions, chopped
12 oz cooking apples, peeled, cored and sliced
salt and pepper
¼ pint cider
¼ pint chicken stock
1½ oz sage and onion stuffing mix, reconstituted

Place the potatoes, pork, onions and two thirds of the apples in a casserole. Sprinkle with salt and pepper.
Pour the cider and stock over the contents of the casserole.
Cover and cook at 325°F (170°C) Gas Mark 3 for 1½ hours. Remove the lid. Spread the reconstituted stuffing mix over the meat and vegetables and decorate with a ring of apple slices.
Return to the oven for a further 25 minutes to cook the apple and stuffing.

Cassoulet

Serves 4

¾ lb white haricot beans, soaked overnight
2 stock cubes
1 large onion, roughly chopped
1 lb potatoes, peeled and cubed
4 oz salami, diced
1¼ lb lean pork, cut into 1 inch cubes
salt and pepper
1 × 15 oz can tomatoes
¼ pt stock
1 teaspoon made mustard

Dissolve the stock cubes in a large saucepan of boiling water. Plunge the beans into the water, reduce the heat and simmer gently for 1½ hours. Drain.
Mix the haricot beans, onion, potatoes, salami and pork together in a large casserole. Season.
Add the tomatoes.
Dissolve the mustard in the stock and pour over the contents of the casserole.
Cover and cook at 350°F (180°C) Gas Mark 4 for 2 hours.

Sausage Casserole

12 oz cabbage, shredded
2 onions, sliced
12 oz tomatoes, skinned and
    quartered
1½ lb chipolata sausages
4 oz bacon, derinded and chopped
1 tablespoon cornflour
½ pint cider
¼ pint stock
1 tablespoon tomato purée
1 clove garlic, crushed
1 dessertspoon demerara sugar
salt and pepper
1 lb potatoes, peeled and thinly
    sliced
1 tablespoon cooking oil

Mix the cabbage, onions, tomatoes, sausages and bacon together and place in a casserole.

Blend together the cornflour, cider, stock, tomato purée, garlic and sugar. Season to taste and pour over the contents of the casserole.

Cover with overlapping potato slices and brush with the cooking oil.

Cover and cook at 375°F (190°C) Gas Mark 5 for 1 hour.

Remove the cover; increase the heat to 425°F (220°C) Gas Mark 7 and continue cooking for a further 30 minutes to brown the potatoes.

Latkes

1 lb potatoes, grated
1 oz S.R. flour
pinch of salt
1 large egg, beaten
3 tablespoons caster sugar } mixed together
1 teaspoon cinnamon
cooking oil for frying

Squeeze the excess water from the potatoes.

Place them in a bowl with the flour, salt and beaten egg and mix well together.

Coat the base of a frying pan with cooking oil and drop dessertspoonsful of the mixture into the pan.

Fry until golden brown on both sides turning the cakes once only. Drain on kitchen paper.

Dust with the mixed sugar and cinnamon and serve hot.

Successor

THIS INFANT DOG, folded in honeyed fur,
Folded in sleep, paws bunched across her nose,
Artlessly sprawls before the winter fire
And nuzzles close to us who are her world.
Twitching in dreams she lives again the chase,
Her tawny body hurled
Hilariously across the wind-wracked shore;
In dreams scuds after gulls through spume
    and foam
Of teasing tides; perhaps again she hears
The thin lost cries of sandpipers in her ears.

In sleep she stretches, yawns, begins to stir,
The stares with topaz eyes as if she saw
The dog who lay last winter in her place.
She stares and inches close
And offers us a guileless trusting paw,
Claiming us for her own—this dog we chose
To turn a house once more into a home.

Margaret Rhodes

Farmhouse Lamb Pie

1 lb lean shoulder lamb, cubed
1 oz flour
1 tablespoon cooking oil
1 lb potatoes, peeled and cubed
1 × 15 oz tin vegetable soup
½ teaspoon rosemary

Pastry
2 oz butter
2 oz lard
6 oz flour
pinch salt
3 oz potatoes, mashed

Toss the lamb in the flour and fry briskly in the oil until the meat is sealed and browned.

Add the potatoes, soup and rosemary and simmer for 20 minutes. Turn into a pie dish.

Make the pastry by rubbing the fats into the flour. Add a pinch of salt and the mashed potatoes and blend together with a fork adding no liquid whatsoever.

Roll out on a lightly floured board and cover the pie dish with the pastry. Flute the edges with finger and thumb.

Make a slit in the pastry to allow the steam to escape. Brush with a little milk to glaze.

Cook at 375°F (190°C) Gas Mark 5 for 20 minutes, then reduce the heat to 325°F (170°C) Gas Mark 3 and continue cooking for a further 40 minutes.

If the pastry is browning too quickly cover the dish with a sheet of greaseproof paper.

Roly Poly

8 oz potatoes, mashed
2 eggs, hard boiled and chopped
3 oz Cheddar cheese, grated
salt and pepper
1 egg beaten
½ teaspoon mixed herbs
1 lb sausagemeat

Place the potatoes, hard boiled eggs, cheese, salt and pepper in a bowl and add sufficient beaten egg to bind.

Beat the herbs into the sausagemeat and roll into an oblong ½ inch thick on a floured board.

Spread the filling over the meat to within ½ inch of the edges and roll up like a swiss roll.

Lift into a roasting tin. Glaze with the remaining beaten egg and cover loosely with foil.

Cook at 375°F (190°C) Gas Mark 5 for 45 minutes. Remove the foil and continue cooking for a further 20 minutes to brown the roly poly.

Irish Sausages

2 onions, sliced
1 oz butter
1 oz flour
1 teaspoon made mustard
½ pint stout
½ pint stock
1 lb thick beef sausages, lightly fried
4 oz button mushrooms
1 lb potatoes, parboiled and sliced
1 tablespoon cooking oil

Fry the onions in the butter until soft.

Stir in the flour and mustard and cook for 1 minute, gradually add the stout and stock stirring continuously until the sauce comes to the boil. Season.

Place the sausages and button mushrooms in a casserole, then pour the sauce over them.

Cover with overlapping slices of potato. Brush the potatoes with the oil.

Cook at 350°F (180°C) Gas Mark 4 for 50-60 minutes until the potatoes are golden brown.

Caribbean Gammon

Serves 4

4 gammon steaks
1 lb potatoes, boiled
1 oz butter
1 egg, beaten
4 pineapple rings, chopped
1 oz butter
1 oz demerara sugar
2 tablespoons pineapple syrup
pinch of salt

Lightly grill the gammon steaks on both sides, then transfer to a greased baking sheet.

Mash the potatoes with the butter and egg and beat until smooth. Place in a piping bag fitted with a No. 10 star nozzle and cover each gammon steak with piped potato.

Scatter the chopped pineapple rings over the potato.

Place the butter, sugar, pineapple juice and pinch of salt in a small saucepan and simmer for 2-3 minutes until the mixture becomes syrupy. Spoon over the potato covered steaks.

Bake at 425°F (220°C) Gas Mark 7 for 15-20 minutes.

Ham, Cheese and Potato Pie

Serves 4

1¼ lb potatoes, peeled and sliced
1 onion, chopped
salt and pepper
8 oz cooked ham, chopped
6 oz Cheddar cheese, grated
1 egg, beaten
½ pint milk

Arrange a layer of potatoes in the bottom of a well buttered ovenproof dish. Sprinkle with chopped onion and season with salt and pepper.

Cover with a layer of chopped ham then a layer of grated cheese.

Repeat these layers twice more finishing with a thick layer of cheese.

Pour the beaten egg and milk over the contents of the dish.

Cover with a sheet of greaseproof paper and cook at 350°F (180°C) Gas Mark 4 for 1¼-1½ hours until the potatoes are tender.

Remove the greaseproof paper and continue cooking until the top is nicely browned.

Tripe and Onion Supreme

Serves 4

1 lb tripe, plain and honeycomb,
    cut into 1 inch strips
2 medium onions, quartered
2 celery sticks, chopped
¾ pint white stock
1 lb potatoes, peeled and cut into
    chunks
salt and pepper
1 oz butter
1 oz flour
½ pint milk
1 tablespoon parsley, chopped

Scald the tripe and onions in boiling water. Strain and repeat once more.

Place the tripe, onions and celery in a large saucepan with the stock and simmer for 45 minutes.

Add the potatoes plus 1 teaspoon salt and simmer for a further 45 minutes.

Make a sauce by melting the butter, stirring in the flour and cooking for 2 minutes without colouring. Gradually add the milk beating continuously until it comes to the boil.

Drain the liquor from the tripe and add enough of it to the sauce to give a pouring consistency. Season the sauce if necessary.

Place the drained tripe and vegetables in a serving dish, coat with the sauce and garnish with the chopped parsley.

Chicken and Mushroom Pudding

Serves 4

Pastry
4 oz butter
8 oz S.R. flour
½ teaspoon baking powder
pinch salt
6 oz potatoes, peeled and grated

Filling
1 large onion, chopped
1 oz butter
8 oz chicken, cooked and roughly chopped
4 oz bacon, cut into snippets
4 oz mushrooms, sliced
½ oz flour
½ teaspoon mixed herbs
½ pint chicken stock

Rub the butter into the flour until the mixture resembles fine breadcrumbs. Mix in the baking powder, salt and grated potatoes. There should be enough water in the potatoes to bind the pastry, but if not add a few drops of cold water.

Line a greased pudding basin with ⅔ of the pastry. Lay aside while you prepare the filling.

Gently fry the onion in the butter until soft but not coloured. Add the chicken, bacon and mushrooms and continue cooking for another few minutes.

Stir in the flour and herbs; gradually pour in the stock and bring to the boil stirring continuously. Simmer for 2 minutes.

Transfer the contents of the frying pan to the lined pudding basin.

Roll out the remaining pastry to make a lid for the pudding. Seal the edges with water.

Cover securely with aluminium foil or a pudding cloth.

Place in a pan of boiling water and steam gently for 2 hours.

Warwickshire Kidneys

Serves 4

12 kidneys halved and cored
1 oz seasoned flour
3 oz butter
2 large onions, sliced
2 large cooking apples, peeled and sliced
1 lb potatoes, cut into large dice
bouquet garni
¾ pint beef stock
salt and pepper
1 teaspoon cornflour (optional)

Toss the kidneys in the seasoned flour. Fry briskly in 1½ oz butter then place in a large casserole.

Add the remaining butter to the pan and fry the onions gently for 5 minutes.

Add the apples and potatoes and cook for a further 5 minutes. Place in the casserole.

Season with salt and pepper and the bouquet garni. Pour the stock over the contents of the casserole.

Cover and cook at 300°F (150°C) Gas Mark 2 for 1½ hours.

Uncover. Remove the bouquet garni, check the seasoning and if necessary thicken the gravy with a little cornflour slaked in water.

Frying Saucers

Serves 4

1 lb potatoes
1 medium onion, sliced
½ oz butter
2 oz boiled ham, finely chopped
1 tomato skinned, deseeded and finely chopped
1 heaped tablespoon flour
1 egg yolk
1 teaspoon French mustard
salt and pepper
cooking oil for frying

Boil the potatoes and onion together in salted water. Drain and dry over a low heat.

Add all the other ingredients and mix thoroughly. Season to taste.

Cover the base of a frying pan with cooking oil and gently spoon in dessertspoonsful of the mixture.

Fry gently for approximately 7-8 minutes on each side until they are golden brown.

A Snowdrop Glade   Photo: Thomas Henshall

Liver and Potato Lyonnaise

Serves 4

2 oz butter
1 tablespoon cooking oil
1¼ lb potatoes, parboiled and cut
    into slices ¼ inch thick
6 oz onions, thinly sliced
salt and black pepper
12 oz liver
1 oz seasoned flour
⅓ pint milk
1 tablespoon sherry
1 tablespoon parsley, chopped

Heat 1 oz butter and the cooking oil in a frying pan. Add the potatoes, onions and seasoning.

Cook gently until the potatoes are cooked and golden brown, approximately 15 minutes.

Meanwhile cut the liver into bite sized pieces and toss in the seasoned flour.

Fry in the remaining 1 oz butter until cooked. Place in the centre of a serving dish and keep hot.

Stir any remaining flour into the pan juices and cook for 1-2 minutes. Gradually add the milk and sherry stirring constantly. Season with salt and a generous shake of black pepper. Bring to the boil.

Arrange the potatoes round the edge of the serving dish, pour the sauce over the liver and garnish with chopped parsley.

Savoury Potato Torte

Serves 4

2 lb potatoes, boiled
2 oz butter
2 tablespoons milk
1 egg yolk
3 oz cream cheese
1 tablespoon chives, chopped
4 oz luncheon meat, finely chopped
½ clove garlic, crushed
salt and pepper
2 egg whites
dried breadcrumbs

Mash the potatoes with the butter, milk, egg yolk and cream cheese.

Gently stir in the chopped chives, luncheon meat, garlic, salt and pepper.

Whisk the egg whites until they stand in peaks then gently fold into the potatoes.

Pour the mixture into a greased cake tin lined with breadcrumbs.

Cook at 400°F (200°C) Gas Mark 6 for 30 minutes.

Turn out and cut into wedges.

Liver Sausage Flan

Serves 4

1½ lb potatoes, boiled
1 egg, beaten
1 dessertspoon Parmesan cheese
8 oz liver sausage
1 × 8 oz packet frozen chopped
    spinach, defrosted and drained
3 tablespoons single cream
salt and pepper
4 oz Cheshire cheese, grated

Mash the potatoes with the egg and Parmesan cheese.

Line a greased loose bottomed cake or flan tin with the potato mixture. Cook at 400°F (200°C) Gas Mark 6 for 10 minutes. Remove from the oven.

Beat the liver sausage until soft and spread over the base of the potato flan.

Mix together the spinach, cream, salt and pepper and pour over the liver sausage.

Sprinkle with the cheese and return to the oven for a further 20-25 minutes.

Remove carefully from the flan tin and serve while still hot.

Spring

"And wind-flowers and violets which yet join not scent to hue crown the pale year weak and new."

Shelley

Vegetarian Pie

Serves 4

2½ oz butter
1 egg, beaten
1½ lb potatoes, mashed
8 oz mushrooms
4 eggs, hard boiled and sliced
½ pint cheese sauce
1 tablespoon parsley, chopped

Blend 1½ oz butter and the beaten egg into the potatoes.

Spread ⅔ of the potato mixture over the base of an ovenproof dish.

Sauté the mushrooms in the remaining 1 oz butter. Arrange the hard boiled eggs and the mushrooms in the dish, reserving some for use as a garnish. Pour the cheese sauce over the eggs and mushrooms.

Place the remaining potatoes in a piping bag fitted with a No. 10 star nozzle and pipe a wheel design on top of the sauce; the rim of the wheel round the edge of the dish and the spokes radiating from the centre.

Cook at 400°F (200°C) Gas Mark 6 for 30 minutes.

Remove from the oven and garnish with egg slices, mushrooms and chopped parsley.

Photo page 66

Kentish Herring Pie

Serves 4

5 herrings, boned
1 lb potatoes, peeled and sliced
2 large cooking apples, sliced
½ teaspoon tarragon
1 tablespoon lemon juice
salt and pepper
1 oz butter, melted

Cut the herrings in half lengthwise.

Fill a greased dish with alternate layers of herring, potatoes, and apples, sprinkling each layer with tarragon, lemon juice and seasoning. Finish with a layer of potatoes.

Brush the potatoes with the melted butter and cook at 400°F (200°C) Gas Mark 6 for 45-50 minutes until the pie is cooked and the top potatoes are crisp and golden brown.

Photo page 66

Picture shows: Vegetarian Pie, Kentish Herring Pie, Paupiettes of Plaice *(page 68).*

Paupiettes of Plaice

Serves 4

1 lb plaice fillets
1 medium onion
2 oz butter
3 tablespoons tomato purée
3 tablespoons sherry
salt and pepper
¼ pint double cream
1 egg, beaten
1 lb potatoes, mashed
4 oz cheese, grated
sprigs of parsley to garnish

Roll up the plaice fillets and arrange in the centre of a shallow ovenproof dish. Cover with greaseproof paper and place in a fairly hot oven 400°F (200°C) Gas Mark 6 for 15 minutes.

Meanwhile sauté the onion in 1 oz butter until transparent; stir in the tomato purée, sherry, salt, pepper and cream. Keep warm but do not allow the sauce to boil.

Remove the fish from the oven and uncover.

Beat the remaining 1 oz butter and the egg into the potatoes. Place in a piping bag fitted with a No. 10 star nozzle and pipe a double border of potato round the edge of the dish.

Pour the sauce over the fish and top with grated cheese.

Return to the oven and cook for a further 20 minutes until the potato is lightly browned and the cheese has melted.

Garnish with parsley sprigs.   *Photo page 66*

Citrus Pudding

Serves 4

6 oz shortcrust pastry
2 oz butter
2 oz sugar
3 oz potatoes, mashed
grated rind of 1 lemon
1 whole egg and 1 yolk, beaten

Line a 6 inch sandwich or flan tin with the pastry and bake blind at 425°F (220°C) Gas Mark 7 for 10-15 minutes.

Cream the butter and sugar until soft and creamy.

Add the potatoes, lemon rind and eggs and mix well together.

Turn into the pastry case and bake at 350°F (180°C) Gas Mark 4 for 50-60 minutes.

Serve hot with cream.

Curried Drumsticks

Serves 4

2 medium onions, chopped
4 oz cooked ham, cubed
1 lb potatoes, peeled and cut into
    chunks
2 medium eating apples, peeled and
    chopped
1 clove garlic, crushed
2 oz butter
8 chicken drumsticks, skin removed
2 teaspoons curry powder
½ teaspoon thyme
1 bay leaf
½ teaspoon cinnamon
2 tomatoes, peeled and chopped
salt and pepper
¼ pint chicken stock
3 tablespoons double cream
juice of 1 lemon

Gently fry the onions, ham, potatoes, apple and garlic in 1 oz butter for 5-10 minutes. Remove from the pan.

Add a further 1 oz butter, lightly fry the chicken drumsticks then stir in the curry powder.

Return the ham and potato mixture to the pan, add the thyme, bay leaf, cinnamon, tomatoes, salt and pepper.

Pour in the stock and bring to the boil. Cover and simmer for 30-35 minutes.

Uncover and remove the bay leaf.

Stir in the cream and lemon juice and cook gently, without a lid, for 10 minutes to reduce the sauce slightly.

Leek Roll

1 large onion, chopped
1 oz butter
6 oz potatoes, mashed
1 lb minced beef
2 oz white breadcrumbs
½ teaspoon mixed herbs
1 × 5 fl. oz. carton soured cream
salt and pepper
1 oz flour
1 egg, separated
8 oz leeks, chopped
1 tablespoon parsley, chopped

Fry the onion in the butter until soft but not coloured.

In a large bowl mix together the potatoes, mince, breadcrumbs, herbs and 2 tablespoons of the soured cream. Season.

Gradually work in the flour and the egg yolk. At this stage the mixture should be pliable but not sticky.

On a lightly floured board roll out the meat mixture until you have a rectangle ¼ inch thick.

Scatter the leeks over the rectangle to within ½ inch of its long outer edges. Moisten the edges and roll up like a swiss roll.

Beat the egg white until frothy and brush over the meat roll.

Cook at 375°F (190°C) Gas Mark 5 for one hour.

To serve, heat the remainder of the soured cream and add the parsley without allowing the cream to boil. Place the meat roll on a serving plate and pour the cream over the top.

21 March

The Earth
(Or so it seemed to me today)
Began to breathe again:
And clouds,
Lively as lambs,
Danced about the sky.

It was as if
(Or so I thought)
The calendar had drawn
The boundary of Spring
Exactly:
And Winter
Had itself been killed
In a single season-changing night.

But the date of Spring
Should surely be
(Or so I thought)
Just chance.
Like waking, dreaming,
Love, and death—
Essentially unbidden.

And yet today it was not so;
And I felt it strongly:
The warm, giving,
Pregnant earth—
And all the promise.
Unfolding summer
Beckoned me—
And turned the pages
Of my winter-jaded mind.

Tom Salmon

Pan Hash

Serves 4

2 tablespoons oil
1 large onion, chopped
1 clove garlic, crushed
6 oz bacon, derinded and cut into
  strips
1¼ lb potatoes, peeled and thinly
  sliced
salt and pepper

Heat the oil in a frying pan and fry the onion, garlic and bacon briskly for 3-4 minutes.

Add the potatoes and continue frying for a further 3-4 minutes, turning the contents of the pan frequently. Season.

Cover the pan, reduce the heat and simmer gently for 30 minutes.

While the pan hash is cooking occasionally press down the contents of the pan with a spatula.

Turn out onto a serving plate and serve with fried eggs.

Cumbrian Hot Pot

Serves 4

12 oz white cabbage, shredded
8 oz black pudding, cut into chunks
4 oz bacon, derinded and cut into
  strips
1 medium onion sliced
2 tablespoons cooking oil
salt and pepper
¼ pint stock
1¼ lb potatoes, peeled and thinly
  sliced
1 oz butter melted

Plunge the cabbage into boiling salted water for 5 minutes. Drain.

Fry the black pudding, bacon and onion in the cooking oil for 5 minutes.

Add the cabbage and toss until the meat and vegetables are thoroughly mixed. Season.

Turn into a deep casserole. Pour in the stock.

Top with a layer of overlapping potato slices. Brush with melted butter.

Cover and cook at 325°F (170°C) Gas Mark 3 for 1½ hours. Remove the lid for the last 15 minutes of cooking time to brown the potatoes slightly.

Potato and Bacon Omelette

Serves 4

4 oz streaky bacon, derinded
  and chopped
1 medium onion, chopped
12 oz potatoes, boiled and cut into
  slices ¼ inch thick
salt and pepper
6 eggs, beaten

Put the bacon in a frying pan and fry briskly until the bacon fat runs.

Reduce the heat, add the onions and the potatoes, and cook gently until they are golden brown. Season.

Pour the beaten eggs over the contents of the frying pan and continue cooking, shaking the pan occasionally. When the eggs are set on the underside, place the frying pan under a hot grill to set and flash the top of the omelette.

Cut into wedges to serve.

Sausage Supper

Serves 4

1 large onion, chopped
1 oz butter
1½ lb potatoes, boiled
2 tablespoons cream
½ teaspoon mixed herbs
1 teaspoon made mustard
black pepper
1 lb thick sausages

Fry the onion in the butter until soft and light brown in colour.

Mash the potatoes with the cream, mixed herbs and mustard.

Fold in the fried onions and season well with black pepper.

Turn into a shallow fireproof dish and arrange the sausages on top of the potato mixture.

Cook at 375°F (180°C) Gas Mark 5 for 40-45 minutes until the sausages are nicely browned.

Peachy Chicken

4 chicken quarters
1 oz butter, melted
1 × 15 oz tin peach halves

Sauce

1 tablespoon honey
2 teaspoons French mustard
1 tablespoon Worcestershire sauce
2 tablespoons vinegar
2 tablespoons peach juice from the tin of peaches
½ teaspoon salt

Potato Pancake

1 lb potatoes, peeled and thinly sliced
2 oz butter
salt and black pepper

Brush the chicken pieces with the melted butter and put into a roasting tin.

Combine all the sauce ingredients together and pour over the chicken pieces.

Cook at 350°F (180°C) Gas Mark 4 for 1 hour, basting frequently. Add the peach halves to the roasting tin 15 minutes before the end of cooking time.

While the chicken is cooking prepare the potato pancake.

Blot the potatoes with kitchen paper.

Rub 1 oz butter over the base and sides of a 6 inch frying pan. Layer the potatoes in the pan seasoning lightly between the layers. Dot with the remaining butter.

Cover and cook over a moderate heat for 10-15 minutes occasionally pressing the potatoes down with a wooden spatula.

After 10-15 minutes the potatoes will have formed a pancake and will be brown on the underside.

Turn carefully and continue cooking for another 10-15 minutes to brown the other side. Transfer to a serving dish.

Arrange the chicken portions and the peaches on top of the potato pancake and spoon the pan juices over the chicken.

Spring—The edge of the Wood Anne Wales Smith

Banger and Bean Hotpot

Serves 4

8 oz haricot beans, soaked overnight
1 lb thick beef sausages, lightly
   grilled
8 oz tomatoes, skinned and
   quartered
1 onion, sliced
1 lb potatoes, peeled and cubed
salt and pepper
¼ pint dry cider
½ pint beef stock
1 tablespoon tomato purée
1 tablespoon cornflour

Simmer the beans in boiling salted water for 1 hour. Drain.

Place in a casserole with the sausages, tomatoes, onion and potatoes. Season.

Blend the cider and the stock into the cornflour and tomato purée, then pour over the contents of the casserole.

Cover and cook at 325°F (170°C) Gas Mark 3 for 1 ½ hours.

Coconut Macaroon Bar

5 oz cooking chocolate
12 oz icing sugar, sifted
3 oz dessicated coconut
3 oz potatoes mashed

Melt the cooking chocolate in a bowl held over a pan of hot water.

Grease a shallow baking tin 8 × 6 inches and coat the base of the tin with half of the chocolate. Lay aside to set.

Gradually work the icing sugar and coconut into the cold mashed potato. Beat for 3-4 minutes.

Press this mixture into the tin and flatten it with a palette knife.

Pour the remainder of the melted chocolate over the macaroon mixture.

Once the chocolate has set cut into 1 inch squares and place in paper sweet cases.

Calypso Ham

Serves 4

1 egg, beaten
1 oz butter, melted
1 lb potatoes, boiled and sieved
2 bananas, halved lengthwise
4 slices boiled ham
¾ oz butter
½ oz flour
½ pint milk
salt and pepper

Beat the egg and melted butter into the potatoes. Place in a piping bag fitted with a No. 10 star nozzle and pipe a double border of duchesse potato round the edge of a shallow fireproof dish.

Roll each halved banana in a slice of boiled ham and arrange in the centre of the dish.

Make a sauce by melting the butter in a saucepan, stirring in the flour and gradually adding the milk stirring continuously until the sauce comes to the boil. Season.

Pour the sauce over the ham and banana rolls, masking them completely.

Cook in a hot oven 400°F (200°C) Gas Mark 6 for 25 minutes.

The Pear Tree

IN May the pear-tree branches
  Blossom and bend low
Under their avalanches
And drifts of snow;

And instantly I remember
How, in the star-blue light
 Of snow in late December,
They blossomed in the night.

Clive Sansom

Bacon Toad

Serves 4

½ oz lard or dripping
12 oz potatoes, cooked and diced
6 oz bacon, grilled and cut into
    snippets

Batter
3 oz flour
pinch salt
1½ oz butter, melted
3 eggs
½ pint milk

Pre-set the oven at 425°F (220°C) Gas Mark 7.

Place the lard or dripping in a roasting tin and heat in the oven until smoking hot.

Meanwhile prepare the batter by beating together the flour, salt, butter and eggs, gradually stir in the milk.

Remove the roasting tin from the oven. Scatter the potatoes and bacon into the fat then pour in the batter.

Return to the oven and cook uncovered for 30-35 minutes until browned and well risen.

Parisienne Kidneys

Serves 4

1½ lb potatoes, peeled
2 tablespoons cooking oil
salt and pepper
1 lb lamb kidneys, skinned and cored
1 oz butter
1 medium onion, chopped
4 oz mushrooms, sliced
1 teaspoon French mustard
1 × 5 fl oz carton soured cream
1 tablespoon parsley, chopped

With a round vegetable or parisienne spoon scoop out balls of potatoes the size of a hazelnut. Rinse in cold water.

Heat the oil in a saucepan. Add the potatoes and season lightly with salt and pepper. Cook over a gentle heat turning frequently until cooked and golden in colour.

Cut the kidneys into bite sized pieces and fry gently in the butter with the onions and mushrooms for 10 minutes. Season.

Blend the mustard with the cream and pour over the kidneys. Heat without boiling.

Arrange the kidney mixture in the centre of a serving dish and surround with the golden potato balls.

Garnish with chopped parsley just before serving.

Princess Lamb Chops

Serves 4

1 lb potatoes, peeled and cut into
    slices ¼ inch thick
1 oz butter
1 medium onion, sliced
salt and pepper
1 × 7 oz tin pimentos
1 tablespoon parsley, chopped
4 lamb chops, trimmed
1 egg, beaten
breadcrumbs for coating
1 tablespoon cooking oil

Boil the potatoes in a pan of salted water for 5 minutes. Drain.

Melt the butter in a frying pan, add the potatoes, onion and seasoning and cook over a gentle heat until the onion is soft and the potatoes are golden brown.

Add the pimentos and parsley and cook for a further 5 minutes.

Meanwhile dip the chops in the beaten egg and coat with breadcrumbs. Fry gently in the oil until cooked and golden brown.

Mound the potato mixture in the centre of a serving dish and arrange the chops round the edge of the platter.

Gingerbread Squares

5 oz wholemeal flour
1 level teaspoon baking powder
1 level teaspoon mixed spice
1 level teaspoon ground ginger
pinch salt
3 oz potatoes, peeled and grated
2 oz mixed peel
2 oz sultanas
2 oz golden syrup
2 oz black treacle
2 oz butter
1 egg, beaten
1 level teaspoon bicarbonate of soda
1 tablespoon water

thin water icing

Line an 11 × 7 inch tin with greased greaseproof paper or foil.

Sieve the flour, baking powder, mixed spice, ground ginger and salt together. Add the potatoes, mixed peel and sultanas and mix well together.

Melt the syrup, treacle and butter together and stir into the mixture with the egg and the bicarbonate of soda dissolved in the water.

Pour into the lined tin and bake at 350°F (180°C) Gas Mark 4 for 30 minutes.

Remove from the tin and cover with thin water icing while still hot.

Allow to cool and cut into squares.

Spanish Liver

Serves 4

1½ lb liver, sliced
12 button onions
2 oz butter
1 lb small potatoes, peeled and
    halved
6 young carrots, scraped
1 oz flour
½ pint chicken stock
½ pint white wine
1 dessertspoon tomato purée
1 teaspoon grated orange rind
1 orange cut into segments

Fry the liver and onions gently in the butter for 5 minutes, then transfer to a casserole with the potatoes and carrots.

Stir the flour into the pan juices and cook for 2-3 minutes. Add the stock, wine, tomato purée and orange rind and bring to the boil stirring constantly. Season.

Pour the sauce over the contents of the casserole.

Cover and cook at 325°F (170°C) Gas Mark 3 for 1-1¼ hours.

Garnish with orange segments before serving.

Planting

Although in a few sheltered spots in the south and west of Britain potatoes are planted very early in the year, the planting generally does not take place until March and April.

Machines have been developed in recent years which plant the seed at even spacings and, whilst doing so, do not damage or remove the very tender sprouts which have formed in readiness to grow into potato plants.

It takes about 2½ tonnes of seed to plant 1 hectare (2½ acres) of land. 1 hectare of planted seed will yield, under favourable growing conditions as much as 50 tonnes of potatoes.

Garlic Sausage Flan

3 eggs, beaten
1 oz butter, melted
6 oz garlic sausage, finely diced
1 lb potatoes, mashed
4 tablespoons single cream
salt and pepper
1 tablespoon chives, chopped

Serves 4

Beat 1 egg, the butter and the garlic sausage into the potatoes.

Grease a shallow loose bottomed 7 inch sponge or flan tin and line the bottom and sides with the potato mixture.

Blend the eggs, cream and seasoning together and pour into the centre of the potato lined flan case. Scatter with chopped chives.

Bake at 375°F (190°C) Gas Mark 5 for 30-35 minutes until the filling has set.

Grenadier Guard

½ oz butter
1 medium onion, finely chopped
1 × 15 oz can tomatoes, drained
salt and pepper
pinch cayenne pepper
½ teaspoon curry powder
few drops Worcestershire sauce
8 oz potatoes, cooked and sliced
   ¼ inch thick
4 oz Cheddar cheese, grated
1 lb thick sausages, grilled

Serves 4

Melt the butter and fry the onion gently for 5 minutes.

Add the tomatoes, salt and pepper, cayenne, curry powder and Worcestershire sauce. Bring to the boil and simmer for a further 5 minutes.

Place the potatoes in the bottom of an ovenproof dish. Cover with the sauce and top with grated cheese.

Cook uncovered at 425°F (220°C) Gas Mark 7 for 20-25 minutes.

Remove from the oven and arrange the sausages on top of the dish in a cartwheel design.

Savoury Surprises

1 × 11½ oz tin corned beef
1½ lb potatoes, mashed
2 tablespoons tomato ketchup
1 medium onion, grated
black pepper
1 oz butter, melted

Serves 4

Cut the corned beef into 8 slices and place on a greased baking sheet.

Beat together the potatoes, ketchup, onion, pepper and half of the butter.

Cover the corned beef slices with the potato mixture and swirl with a fork.

Brush with the remaining butter and cook at 400°F (200°C) Gas Mark 6 for 20-25 minutes until crisp and golden.

Piquant Corned Beef Pie

1 lb potatoes, peeled and quartered
8 oz swede, peeled and cut into
   ½ inch cubes
2 oz butter
1 medium onion chopped
1 oz flour
1 teaspoon curry powder
¼ pint beef stock
1 dessertspoon Worcestershire
   sauce
salt and pepper
12 oz corned beef, diced

Serves 4

Plunge the potatoes and swede into boiling salted water and cook gently for 20 minutes.

Meanwhile melt 1 oz butter and fry the onion until soft. Stir in the flour and curry powder and cook for 1 minute. Gradually add the stock and Worcestershire sauce stirring constantly until the sauce comes to the boil. Season.

Fold in the corned beef and simmer for 5 minutes. Transfer to a greased pie dish.

Drain and dry the potatoes and swede and mash with the remaining 1 oz butter. Cover the corned beef mixture with the mashed potato and swede forking it into a pattern.

Flash under a hot grill.

Paradise Fingers

8 oz shortcrust pastry
apricot or raspberry jam
4 oz butter
4 oz caster sugar
1 egg, beaten
2 oz mashed potatoes
1 oz ground almonds
2 oz ground rice
few drops almond essence
4 oz sultanas
2 oz glace cherries, chopped
2 oz walnuts, chopped

Line a swiss roll tin with the shortcrust pastry and spread thinly with jam.

Cream the butter and sugar together, add the egg and the mashed potatoes and beat until the mixture is light and creamy.

Fold in the other ingredients and spread the mixture over the pastry.

Bake at 350°F (180°C) Gas Mark 4 for 45 minutes until well browned.

Remove from the oven, sprinkle with castor sugar and leave to cool in the tin.

Cut into fingers when cold.

Curried Beef Salad

2 level teaspoons curry powder
1 teaspoon sugar
pinch salt and pepper
½ pint mayonnaise
6 oz cold roast beef, diced
8 oz potatoes, cooked and diced
2 sticks celery, chopped
¼ cucumber, diced but unpeeled
4 pineapple rings, diced
1 small onion, grated
1 small apple, cored and grated
1 teaspoon lemon juice
lettuce leaves

Serves 4

Add the curry powder, sugar, salt and pepper to the mayonnaise.

Toss all the other ingredients with the exception of the lettuce in this sauce and set aside for 2-3 hours to develop the flavour.

Just before serving arrange the salad on a bed of lettuce leaves.

See what I mean. Its no use writing to Martha for a couple of weeks, yet.

Heaven

MY husband and I often walk across country all day looking for wild flowers—not to pick because, out of their setting, half their beauty is lost. In spring we find green hellebore growing in huge clumps on a wide mossy bank that slopes down to a brook where the deer drink. Some of the plants nestle in the roots of trees right at the water's edge; a few early primroses lighten the picture, and we are quite content to lean against a tree and gaze at it. Later the woods are gay with bluebells and yellow archangel, and we know where herb paris and bird's-nest orchids grow. In summer the meadows are full of flowers, and one here and there may be a haze of pink with fragrant orchids. Once at the end of such a day I called to a jolly-looking farmer and asked him the way to the nearest village. With hat held high in the air and an enormous grin on his face he said, 'Wass zay, maid? Theet lost? Course theet lost. This is heaven out yur. Never thought theet git there, diss?' He could not have expressed our feelings more exactly.

Violet Ricketts, Somerset.

Potato and Celery Soup

Serves 4

2 oz butter
1 lb potatoes, peeled and cut into
   chunks
2 onions, peeled and quartered
5 celery sticks, chopped
1½ pints stock
salt and pepper
¼ pint milk
celery leaves to garnish

Melt the butter and fry the vegetables over a gentle heat for 4-5 minutes.

Add the stock, salt and pepper. Bring to the boil, cover and simmer for 40 minutes.

Sieve or liquidise the soup. Add the milk and reheat, adjusting the seasoning if necessary.

Garnish with a few chopped celery leaves.

Photo page 79

Lamb Meat Balls

Serves 4

Meat Balls

12 oz potatoes, peeled and grated
1 lb minced lamb
1 medium onion, chopped
salt and pepper
1 tablespoon cooking oil for frying

Sauce

1 oz butter
1 large onion, chopped
4 oz mushrooms, sliced
1 oz flour
1 dessertspoon paprika pepper
1 × 7 oz can tomatoes
1 dessertspoon tomato purée
¼ pint stock
salt and pepper
4 tablespoons cream

Make the meatballs by squeezing the excess water from the grated potatoes and combining all the ingredients together. Season.

Roll into balls just a little bigger than a walnut.

Heat the oil and fry the meatballs gently for 10-12 minutes, turning them frequently.

Make the sauce by melting the butter in a saucepan and sautéing the onions and mushrooms until tender. Remove from the pan and keep hot.

Stir into the pan juices the flour, paprika pepper, tomatoes, tomato purée, stock, salt and pepper and continue cooking until the sauce thickens.

Return the onions and mushrooms to the pan and add the cream. Reheat but do not allow the sauce to boil.

Pour over the meatballs and serve with creamed potatoes.

Photo page 79

Beef and Potato Pasties

Potato Pastry

3 oz butter
8 oz potatoes, boiled and sieved
5 oz flour
1 teaspoon baking powder
½ teaspoon salt

Filling

8 oz minced beef
1 large potato, grated
1 large onion, grated
1 carrot, grated
1 tablespoon tomato purée
1 egg, beaten
salt and pepper

Make the pastry by creaming the butter until soft. Add the other ingredients and blend together to form a smooth dough.

Turn onto a floured board and knead lightly. Roll out thinly and using a saucer as a guide cut into rounds.

Make the filling by browning the mince in its own fat. Add the other ingredients and stir over a gentle heat for 3-4 minutes.

Divide the mixture between the pastry rounds. Dampen the edges of the pastry circles, fold over to form pasties and flute the edges. Brush with egg or milk.

Cook at 375°F (190°C) Gas Mark 5 for 30-40 minutes until golden brown.

Photo page 79

Picture shows: Potato and Celery Soup, Lamb Meat Balls, Liver Stroganoff *(page 81)*, Beef and Potato Pasties.

Lettuce and Potato Soup

Serves 4

1 large onion, finely chopped
2 oz butter
12 oz potatoes, peeled and sliced
1¾ pints chicken stock
salt and pepper
1 large lettuce, finely shredded

Sauté the onion in the butter for 3 minutes until soft and transparent.
Add the potatoes, stock and seasoning.
Bring to the boil and simmer for 30 minutes.
Add the finely shredded lettuce and simmer for a further 5-7 minutes.
Sieve or liquidise the soup. Return to the pan, check the seasoning and reheat before serving.

Photo page 2

Dauphine Baskets

Serves 4

Dauphine Potatoes

3 eggs
2½ oz butter
1 lb potatoes, boiled and sieved
¼ pint water
2½ oz flour

Filling

½ oz butter
½ oz flour
½ pint milk
12 oz smoked white fish, cooked and flaked
1 tablespoon parsley, chopped
salt and pepper

Beat one egg and 1 oz butter into the sieved potato.
Place the water and the remaining butter in a saucepan and bring to the boil. Immediately add the flour and beat well until the mixture is smooth. Remove from the heat. Beat the two remaining eggs and stir into the saucepan.
Turn into a bowl with the potatoes and again beat until thoroughly blended.
Place the mixture in a piping bag fitted with a No. 10 star nozzle. On a greased baking tray pipe a circular base about 2½ inch diameter, then build up the sides to form a basket.
Repeat to make 3 more baskets.
With the remaining mixture pipe 4 × 1 inch rounds.
Bake in a hot oven 425°F (220°C) Gas Mark 7 for 10 minutes. Reduce the heat to 375°F (190°C) Gas Mark 5 and continue baking for a further 20 minutes until well risen and golden brown.
Prepare the filling by melting the butter, adding the flour and cooking for 1 minute without browning. Gradually add the milk, stirring constantly until the sauce boils.
Fold in the fish and parsley. Season.
Divide the filling between the four baskets. Place the small rounds on top to look like little lids.
Serve piping hot.

Photo page 2

Kidney Soup

Serves 4

1 oz butter
8 oz kidneys, skinned, cored and chopped
1 large onion, finely chopped
8 oz carrots, grated
6 oz swede, grated
2 pints beef stock
12 oz potatoes, mashed
salt and pepper
2 tablespoons sherry (optional)

Melt the butter in a large pan and toss the kidneys, onion, carrots and swede in the butter for 5 minutes without colouring the vegetables.
Gradually blend the stock into the potatoes then add to the saucepan. Season.
Cover and simmer for 50-60 minutes.
The sherry, if used, should be added just before serving.

Liver Stroganoff

Serves 1

1 tablespoon cooking oil
1 medium onion, finely chopped
4 oz mushrooms, sliced
1 lb lamb's liver, cut into strips
1 × 5 fl oz carton natural yoghurt
1 teaspoon cornflour
1 oz butter, melted
1 egg, beaten
1 lb potatoes, mashed
2 tablespoons parsley, chopped

Heat the oil and fry the onion and mushrooms gently for 5-8 minutes.

Add the liver and fry for another 5 minutes.

Blend the yoghurt with the cornflour and stir into the liver. Cook gently for 2-3 minutes.

Meanwhile beat the butter and egg into the potatoes until smooth. Place the mixture in a piping bag fitted with a No. 10 star nozzle and pipe a border of potato round the edge of a shallow fireproof dish.

Flash under a hot grill to brown the potatoes.

Pile the liver mixture into the centre of the potato border and scatter with chopped parsley.

Photo page 79

Sage and Onion Puffs

8 oz potatoes, grated
1 rounded tablespoon dry sage and
    onion stuffing mix, reconstituted
1 oz S.R. flour
1 egg, beaten
salt and pepper
Cooking oil for deep frying

Squeeze the excess water from the potatoes.

Blend all the ingredients together and beat until thoroughly mixed.

Drop dessertspoonsful of the mixture into hot deep fat and fry for 5-6 minutes until golden brown.

Drain on kitchen paper.

Fragment on childhood

By John Clare

Childhood what a glorious boon
Sweet as mayday's morning sun
Sweet as April's budding blooms
Ere the sunny summer comes
Sweet as June's gay honey showers
Are wild youth's delightful hours
Never dull but ever gay
Always seeking after play
Chucking up the bouncing ball
By bee haunted cottage wall.

Leveret

Orange Potato Balls

1 lb potatoes, boiled
1 oz butter
finely grated rind of 1 orange
2 teaspoons parsley, chopped
salt and pepper
3 tablespoons milk
2 oz flour
1 egg, beaten
golden breadcrumbs for coating
cooking oil for deep frying

Mash the potatoes with the butter, orange rind and parsley. Season.
Allow to cool slightly then form into 12 balls.
Roll the balls in the milk then in the flour.
Dip in the beaten egg then toss in the breadcrumbs until well coated.
Fry in hot deep fat until golden brown.
These orange balls are delicious served with fried white fish.

Carrot and Potato Ragoût

Serves 4

1 lb carrots, cut into strips
1 lb potatoes, peeled and cubed
8 oz button onions
8 oz button mushrooms
4 oz bacon, derinded and cut into strips
2 oz butter
salt and pepper
½ pint stock
1 dessertspoon tomato purée
2 tablespoons sherry
1 dessertspoon arrowroot
1 tablespoon parsley, chopped

Sauté the carrots, potatoes, onions, mushrooms and bacon in the butter for 5 minutes.
Add the seasoning and stock and simmer for 35-40 minutes until the vegetables are tender.
Remove the vegetables to a serving dish and keep warm.
Boil the pan juices rapidly to reduce by half. Blend the tomato purée and sherry into the arrowroot and stir into the pan. Bring to the boil, stirring continuously until the sauce thickens.
Pour over the vegetables and garnish with chopped parsley.

Scalloped Rosemary Potatoes

Serves 4

1½ lb potatoes, peeled and thinly
   sliced
1 large onion, sliced
1 teaspoon rosemary, crushed
salt and pepper
½ pint milk
1½ oz white breadcrumbs
2 oz butter

Arrange the potatoes and onion slices in alternate layers in a greased ovenproof casserole, seasoning well with rosemary, salt and pepper.
Pour the milk over the potatoes and onion. Sprinkle with breadcrumbs and dot with butter.
Cover and cook at 350°F (180°C) Gas Mark 4 for 1½ hours until the milk has been absorbed. The lid should be removed for at least 15 minutes of cooking time to brown the top slightly.

Devilled Potatoes

Serves 4

1 level tablespoon curry powder
2 level tablespoons flour
1 teaspoon dry mustard
pinch salt
1 teaspoon cayenne pepper
1 lb potatoes, cooked and sliced
   ¼ inch thick
3 tablespoons cooking oil

Mix the curry powder, flour, mustard, salt and cayenne pepper together.
Toss the sliced potatoes in the mixed seasoning.
Heat the oil in a frying pan and fry the potatoes over a moderate heat for 10-15 minutes, turning frequently, until crisp and golden brown.

Irish Potato Cakes

8 oz S.R. flour
1 teaspoon baking powder
½ teaspoon salt
1 oz butter
8 oz potatoes, mashed
¼ pint milk

Sieve the flour, baking powder and salt into a bowl; rub in the butter.

Blend in the potatoes and milk to form a dough. Knead until smooth.

Roll out to ¼ inch thick and cut into rounds with a scone cutter.

Fry over a moderate heat in a greased frying pan or griddle for 3-4 minutes on each side. Serve hot.

These potato cakes are delicious served with fried bacon and tomatoes.

Fish Pie De Luxe

Serves 4

1 lb smoked haddock or cod
4 tablespoons milk
1 oz butter
1 oz flour
¼ pint apple juice
2 tablespoons parsley, chopped
4 eggs, hardboiled and chopped
salt and pepper
1½ lb small potatoes, parboiled
2 tablespoons cooking oil

Poach the fish gently in the milk for 3 minutes, drain, reserving the milk.

Melt the butter in a saucepan; stir in the flour and cook for 1 minute. Gradually add the milk in which the fish was poached and the apple juice, stirring continuously until the sauce reaches boiling point.

Flake the fish and fold it into the sauce along with the parsley and the hardboiled eggs. Season to taste.

Turn into a shallow greased ovenproof dish.

Arrange the potatoes round the edge of the dish and brush liberally with the oil.

Cook in a hot oven 400°F (200°C) Gas Mark 6 for 30-35 minutes until the potatoes are nicely browned.

If the exposed fish is browning too quickly cover with a sheet of greaseproof paper.

Untimely Aid

THE cottage, an isolated one in territory new to me, was encircled by a high hedge and had a solid wooden gate. A pleasant-looking old man stood behind this, fumbling with the catch; and as I drew level he raised his head in greeting, mentioning also the fact that he could not untie the string which kept the latch fastened. I appreciated his difficulty, for I had often been held up at my own gate by the knots which kept my small boy from straying on to the road; so I undid the string and threw the gate wide for the old gentleman. Out he stepped, arrayed in Sunday jacket, ancient bowler and long white underpants. As I stood rooted to the spot he turned to me, bowed courteously and, raising his bowler with a smile, said, 'Thank you; good day, ma'am', before setting off briskly up the road. I learnt too late that his long-suffering daughter-in-law, hoping to deter the old eccentric from his wanderings, not only kept the gate tied but hid his trousers, too.—M. Leggott, Yorkshire.

Sunlight in the village

The morning strikes the street with fire,
And windows bloom with flowers of light;
The weathercock upon the spire,
Quickened by sun, bursts into flight.

The swiftly-running tide explores
The huddled houses, dark and deep:
Leaping through keyholes, under doors,
Or resting in a honeyed sleep.

And to the tombstones' ghostly names,
Shadowed by Time and life's rejection,
The trumpet of the sun proclaims
The hope of love and resurrection.

Douglas Gibson

Potato Bake

Serves 4

2 oz butter
1 large onion, chopped
½ pint single cream
1 level tablespoon tomato purée
1 level teaspoon salt
freshly ground black pepper
1½ lb potatoes, grated
4 oz grated cheese

Melt the butter in a frying pan and cook the onion gently until soft and transparent.

Stir in the cream, tomato purée, salt and a generous shake of black pepper. Bring to the boil.

Add the grated potatoes and stir over a gentle heat to warm the mixture.

When it is heated through turn it into a shallow ovenproof dish and sprinkle the top with the grated cheese.

Cook at 400°F (200°C) Gas Mark 6 for 35-40 minutes.

Cup Snack

Serves 1

½ oz butter
1 oz Cheshire cheese, grated
2 oz potatoes, cooked and diced
1 egg
1 tablespoon milk
salt and pepper
1 slice hot buttered toast

Grease a teacup with butter and sprinkle half the cheese into the bottom of the cup. Add the potatoes.

Whisk together the egg, milk, salt and pepper. Pour into the cup.

Sprinkle the remaining cheese on top.

Cover with aluminium foil and place the cup in a pan of gently boiling water which comes halfway up the side of the cup.

Cook for 12-15 minutes until the egg is set. Loosen round the edge and unmould onto the hot buttered toast.

Potato Galette

Serves 4

1 medium onion, finely chopped
2 oz butter
1¼ lb potatoes, mashed
1 egg, beaten
5 oz Cheshire cheese, grated
½ teaspoon made mustard
salt and pepper

Sauté the onion in 1 oz butter until soft and transparent.

Stir the onion into the potatoes, egg, cheese, mustard and seasoning.

Spread the potato mixture into a greased, loose bottomed 7 inch sandwich or flan tin and swirl the top with a fork. Dot with the remaining butter.

Cook uncovered at 375°F (190°C) Gas Mark 5 for 35 minutes until crisp and golden.

Turn out and cut into wedges.

Irish Eggs

Serves 4

1 lb potatoes, mashed
4 eggs, hard boiled and chopped
½ bunch spring onions, chopped
4 oz Cheddar cheese, grated
pinch dry mustard
salt and pepper
1 oz seasoned flour
1 egg, beaten
golden breadcrumbs for coating
deep fat for frying

Mix the potatoes, eggs, spring onions, cheese, mustard and seasoning together.

Divide the mixture into 8 balls. Roll each ball in seasoned flour, dip in the beaten egg and coat with breadcrumbs.

Deep fry in hot fat for 10-12 minutes until golden brown.

Hen's Nests

4 oz Cheddar cheese, finely grated
½ teaspoon made mustard
1 egg, beaten
1 oz butter
1½ lb potatoes, mashed
4 eggs, hard boiled
4 slices processed cheese

Add the cheese, mustard, beaten egg and butter to the potatoes and beat until smooth. Put into a piping bag fitted with a No. 10 star nozzle and pipe 4 potato nests about 2½ inches in diameter.

Place a hard boiled egg in each nest and cover with a slice of cheese, tucking the corners into the sides of the nest.

Flash under a hot grill until the cheese melts and coats the eggs.

Vegetarian Soufflé

Serves 4

4 oz onions, finely chopped
1 oz butter
1½ lb potatoes, mashed
2 oz mature Cheddar cheese, grated
salt and pepper
pinch nutmeg
¼ pint boiling milk
3 eggs, separated
chopped chives and paprika pepper
    to garnish

Gently fry the onions in the butter until soft and transparent.

Mix together the potatoes, cheese, salt, pepper and nutmeg.

Gradually add the boiling milk and mix thoroughly. Stir in the onions and the egg yolks.

Beat the egg whites until stiff and fold into the potato mixture.

Place in a greased soufflé dish and cook at 400°F (200°C) Gas Mark 6 for 30-35 minutes until risen and well browned.

Garnish with chives and paprika pepper.

Pilchard Quiche

Serves 8

6 oz shortcrust pastry
1 × 15 oz tin pilchards in tomato
    sauce
2 eggs, beaten
3 tablespoons milk or single cream
2 tablespoons parsley, chopped
salt and pepper
12 oz potatoes, parboiled and diced

Roll out the pastry and line an 8 inch flan tin or flan ring. Bake blind for 10 minutes at 400°F (200°C) Gas Mark 6.

Meanwhile mash the pilchards until smooth. Beat in the eggs, milk or cream, parsley, salt and pepper. Fold in the potatoes.

Remove the flan case from the oven and fill with the pilchard and potato mixture.

Return to the oven and cook at 350°F (180°C) Gas Mark 4 for 50-55 minutes until the filling is set.

Potato and Tuna Soufflé

Serves 4

1½ lb potatoes, mashed
1 × 7 oz tin tuna fish
1 small onion, finely chopped
1 tablespoon parsley, chopped
3 oz cheese, grated
1 medium red pepper, deseeded and
    finely chopped
4 tablespoons milk
salt and pepper
3 eggs, separated
3 oz flour
½ teaspoon mixed herbs

Mix together the potatoes, tuna, onion, parsley, cheese, red pepper and milk. Season to taste.

Place in a greased casserole and cook at 400°F (200°C) Gas Mark 6 for 20 minutes. Remove from the oven.

Beat the egg whites until stiff. Gently fold the egg yolks, flour, a good pinch of salt and the mixed herbs into the egg whites.

Spread this topping over the potato mixture and return the casserole to the oven for a further 10-12 minutes until the soufflé is well risen and golden brown.

Rainbow Trout En Croute

4 prepared rainbow trout
1 lb puff pastry
1 egg, beaten
1 small bunch watercress
1 lemon

Stuffing

8 oz potatoes, mashed
rind and juice of 1 lemon
1 dessertspoon chives, chopped
1 dessertspoon tarragon, chopped
1 tablespoon parsley, chopped
1 teaspoon powdered mace
salt and pepper

Blend all the stuffing ingredients together and use to fill the four trout.

Roll the pastry out thinly and cut into four rectangles. Place a trout in the centre of each rectangle; season with salt, pepper and a squeeze of lemon juice.

Dampen the pastry edges and fold up neatly over the fish, making the join into an ornamental roll. Brush with beaten egg.

Lay the four trout parcels on a baking sheet and bake at 400°F (200°C) Gas Mark 6 for 20 minutes. Reduce the heat to 350°F (180°C) Gas Mark 4 and continue cooking for a further 25 minutes.

If the pastry browns too quickly cover with a sheet of greaseproof paper or foil.

Garnish with watercress and lemon wedges.

Savoury Mince Loaf

Serves 4

1 lb minced beef
1 medium onion, chopped
1 tablespoon cooking oil
1 tablespoon curry powder
1 × 8 oz can tomatoes
salt
freshly ground black pepper
finely grated rind of 1 lemon
12 oz potatoes, peeled and grated
3 eggs, beaten

Lightly brown the beef and onion in the hot oil.

Stir in the curry powder, tomatoes and seasoning. Simmer for 5 minutes making sure that the tomatoes are well broken down.

Blend in the lemon rind, potatoes and eggs.

Turn into a foil lined loaf tin and cook at 350°F (180°C) Gas Mark 4 for 1-1¼ hours until the loaf is firm to the touch and nicely browned.

Unmould carefully and remove the aluminium foil.

Serve hot or cold.

Greek Steak

Serves 4

1 lb rump steak, cut into 1 inch cubes
1 oz seasoned flour
1 tablespoon cooking oil
12 oz potatoes, peeled and cubed
8 oz carrots, sliced
1 onion, sliced
1 red pepper, deseeded and sliced
salt and pepper
2 tablespoons honey
1 tablespoon lemon juice
4 tablespoons tomato ketchup
½ pint beef stock

Toss the steak in seasoned flour and brown the meat on all sides in the hot oil.

Add the potatoes, carrots, onion and red pepper and continue cooking for another 5 minutes. Shake the pan occasionally to prevent the vegetables sticking. Season.

Mix the honey, lemon juice, tomato ketchup and stock together, and pour over the meat and vegetables.

Cover with a tight fitting lid and simmer for 1¾-2 hours.

Serve with a green vegetable.

Cranberry Pork

2 large onions, sliced
1 oz butter
1¼ lb pork, cut into 1 inch cubes
2 level tablespoons tomato purée
8 oz cranberry jelly
1 teaspoon curry powder
1 lb potatoes, cut into chunks
½ pint stock
salt and pepper

Dumplings

4 oz S.R. flour
1 oz grated potato
2 oz shredded suet
1 tablespoon parsley, chopped
½ teaspoon salt

Fry the onions gently in the butter until golden, remove from the pan.

Increase the heat and brown the pork cubes on all sides.

Return the onions to the pan and stir in the tomato purée, cranberry jelly and curry powder.

Add the potatoes and pour in the stock. Season to taste.

Bring to the boil and simmer for 1¼ hours.

Prepare the dumplings by blending all the ingredients together and adding water gradually until a soft dough is formed.

Divide into 8 portions and roll into balls.

Drop the dumplings into the pork stew for the last 20 minutes of cooking time.

Pulling Together

L AST year in Devon I saw four magnificent horses pulling a wagon loaded with a large oak. Three were Suffolk punches and the fourth, bigger and stronger, a black shire which must have been every bit of eighteen hands. They seemed unable to pull their load up the slightly softer ground leading from a field to the lane, and I half expected a caterpillar tractor to be fetched to the rescue. But the wagoner removed the black, tied it to the hedge and returned to the others. Then, holding the gear horse, he urged them on, and to my surprise the three of them pulled the load into the lane with apparent ease. The wagoner explained that the black shire, though superior in physique and pulling power, was a newcomer to the team, whereas the other three had worked together a good deal. 'It's not a matter of pulling,' he told me, 'but of pulling together'.

Barrie J. Kaye

Watchmaker

Last of his line, the watchmaker is dead,
His shop in the village street will soon close,
Another, of this generation, will be opened instead,
'Boutique' or 'Bookmaker', who knows?

Passing his window I used to see him there,
Head bowed over bench, all hours of the day,
Squatting uncomfortably on edge of old chair,
Jeweller's glass in eye, working away.

Peering at dusty pivots until the light went,
With tiny tweezers lifted out cylinder and wheel,
Fingers tense, forehead furrowed with intent,
Dropped oil on each centimetre of steel.

Cigarette dangling, he cursed the small enginry,
Muttered because an escapement would not come right,
Then, to set pinions to their correct degree,
Put on his spectacles, switched on the light.

Strange, though, he was never on time himself,
Uncertain when jobs were ready, would nervously grope
Among his clutter of parts lying on littered shelf;
You left your watch with him in faith and hope.

Would say 'It will be ready, sir, early next week',
Dismissing you gently, disarm with broad smiles,
Knowing you belonged to the company of the meek,
Went back to fiddling with faces and dials.

His hour now struck, he travels out of time,
His seventy years a hairspring, his clock unwound,
His last watch kept, he hears another chime
Where no chronology is ever found.

Leonard Clark

Wellington Lamb

4 oz potatoes, grated
1 × 15 oz tin peach slices (do not drain)
8 oz sausagemeat
½ teaspoon mixed herbs
salt and pepper
1½ lb breast of lamb, boned weight
2 medium onions, chopped
3 celery sticks, chopped
1 lb potatoes, peeled and cubed
¼ pint chicken stock
3 tablespoons double cream
1 tablespoon parsley, chopped

Squeeze the excess water from the grated potatoes.

Chop 4 peach slices and mix with the grated potatoes, sausagemeat and mixed herbs. Season.

Spread this filling over the breast of lamb and roll up like a swiss roll. Cut into four noisettes and secure each noisette with a wooden cocktail stick.

Brown quickly in their own fat in a non-stick frying pan, then transfer to a shallow ovenproof casserole.

Add the onions, celery and cubed potatoes to the meat.

Pour the stock and ¼ pint of juice from the tin of peaches over the contents of the casserole. Season to taste.

Cover and cook at 350°F (180°C) Gas Mark 4 for 1¼ hours.

Remove the noisettes to a serving dish and keep warm.

Stir the cream, parsley and the remaining peach slices into the casserole. Adjust the seasoning and return to the oven for 5 minutes to heat the peaches.

Pour the contents of the casserole over the lamb noisettes and serve piping hot.

Lamb Goulash

Serves 4

1½ lb shoulder of lamb (boned weight) cut into 1 inch cubes
2 oz seasoned flour
2 tablespoons cooking oil
2 onions, sliced
4 tomatoes, skinned and quartered
1 lb potatoes, peeled and cut into chunks
salt
1 dessertspoon paprika pepper
¾ pint beef stock
¼ pint red wine
3 tablespoons soured cream
1 tablespoon parsley, chopped

Toss the lamb in the seasoned flour.

Heat the oil in a frying pan and brown the meat on all sides, transfer to a casserole.

Reduce the heat and sauté the onions until soft, transfer to the casserole.

Add the tomatoes and potatoes to the meat and onions and mix thoroughly. Season with salt and paprika pepper.

Pour in the stock and wine.

Cover and cook at 325°F (170°C) Gas Mark 3 for 1¾ hours.

Just before serving stir in the soured cream and parsley.

Veal Burgers

Serves 4

8 oz potatoes, grated
8 oz veal, minced
1 teaspoon oregano
salt and pepper
1 oz flour
1 egg, beaten
2 tablespoons cooking oil

Squeeze the excess water from the potatoes.

Add all the other ingredients with the exception of the oil and mix until thoroughly blended.

Heat the oil in a frying pan and drop tablespoonsful of the mixture into the shallow fat, flattening each burger with the back of a spoon.

Fry gently for 7-8 minutes on each side.

Serve with gravy or brown sauce.

Taunton Temptation

Serves 4

1 lb boneless pork
1 oz seasoned flour
1 tablespoon cooking oil
1 large onion, sliced
2 large cooking apples, peeled,
  cored and sliced
1 teaspoon mixed herbs
salt and pepper
½ pint medium cider
1½ lb potatoes, peeled and thinly
  sliced
1 oz butter, melted

Cut the pork into bite sized pieces and toss in the seasoned flour.

Heat the oil in a frying pan and brown the meat on all sides. Transfer to a casserole.

Fry the onion gently for 5 minutes. Add the apples, herbs, salt, pepper and cider. Bring to the boil then pour over the pork in the casserole.

Arrange the potatoes in overlapping slices on top and brush with melted butter.

Cover and cook at 350°F (180°C) Gas Mark 4 for 1¼ hours. Remove the lid, increase the heat to 425°F (220°C) Gas Mark 7 and continue cooking for a further 15 minutes to brown the potatoes.

Top Stuffed Pork Chops

Serves 4

4 pork chops, trimmed
4 dessertspoons single cream

Stuffing

8 oz potatoes, boiled
1 egg yolk
1 small cooking apple, peeled and
  grated
1 small onion, grated
4 tenderised prunes, chopped
1 tablespoon parsley, chopped
salt and pepper

Place the pork chops in a greased roasting tin.

Prepare the stuffing by mashing the potatoes and egg yolk together until smooth. Blend in all the other ingredients. Season.

Spread the stuffing over the chops and pour a dessertspoonful of cream over each one.

Cover the dish securely with foil and cook at 375°F (190°C) Gas Mark 5 for 45-50 minutes.

Remove the foil about 15 minutes before the end of cooking time to brown the stuffing.

Hickory Dicks

Serves 4

8 oz potatoes, grated
1 × 8 oz tin apricot halves, drained
  and chopped
8 oz cooked chicken, finely chopped
2 oz S. R. flour
1 egg, beaten
salt and pepper
deep fat for frying

Squeeze the excess water from the potatoes.

Add the apricots, chicken, flour, egg, salt and pepper; mix thoroughly.

Drop dessertspoonsful of the mixture into hot deep fat and fry for 5 minutes until crisp and golden brown.

Porc au Moutarde

Serves 4

1 lb stewing pork
2 tablespoons cooking oil
1 lb potatoes, cut into 1 inch cubes
4 oz bacon, diced
1 large onion, chopped
4 oz mushrooms, sliced
1 oz flour
½ pint chicken stock
½ pint white wine
1 tablespoon French mustard
salt and black pepper

Fry the pork briskly in the oil until golden brown. Transfer to a casserole along with the potatoes.

Fry the bacon, onion and mushrooms in the same fat until lightly coloured, add to the casserole.

Stir the flour into the pan juices, then blend in the stock, wine and mustard. Season. Pour over the contents of the casserole.

Cover and cook at 325°F (170°C) Gas Mark 3 for 2 hours.

Thursday Pie

Serves 4

¾ oz butter
¾ oz flour
generous pinch of dry mustard
¾ pint milk
salt and pepper
1¼ lb potatoes, boiled and sliced
    ¼ inch thick
8 oz garden peas, cooked
1 lb beef sausages
4 oz cheese, grated

Melt the butter in a saucepan, stir in the flour and mustard and gradually add the milk, stirring continuously until the sauce comes to the boil. Season.

Gently fold the potatoes and peas into the sauce without breaking up the potatoes. Simmer gently for 5 minutes.

Grill the sausages until lightly browned and arrange in the bottom of a fairly shallow ovenproof dish.

Spoon the potato mixture over the sausages and top with the grated cheese.

Flash under a hot grill until the cheese bubbles.

Barbecued Potato an' Sausage

Serves 4

1 lb thick pork sausages
1 tablespoon cooking oil
1 lb potatoes, peeled and cut into
    large dice
1 medium onion, chopped
2 level tablespoons flour
½ pint water
2 level tablespoons sweet pickle
2 level tablespoons tomato ketchup
2 tablespoons vinegar
1 dessertspoon Worcestershire
    sauce
1 level teaspoon made mustard
salt and pepper

Fry the sausages briskly in the oil until browned. Remove from the pan and keep warm.

Reduce the heat and fry the potatoes and onion gently until golden.

Blend the flour into the pan juices and cook for 1 minute. Gradually add the water stirring constantly.

Stir in the sweet pickle, tomato ketchup, vinegar, Worcestershire sauce and made mustard. Season with salt and pepper and bring to the boil.

Return the sausages to the pan.

Cover and simmer gently for 30 minutes.

Stoat

Mark Burgess

POTATOES AS AN ACCOMPANIMENT

"The Proof of the Potato is in the Eating"

Whether they be boiled, mashed, roast or chipped, good potatoes can be spoiled by poor preparation.
Follow these hints and recipes for the best results.

CONSULT the British Potato Wall chart and choose a variety suitable for the purpose.
POTATOES should be peeled very thinly to avoid waste and the valuable nutrients which lie directly under the skin.
POTATOES of even size, will finish cooking at the same time. Cut large potatoes into halves or quarters.
POTATOES require gentle cooking in only enough water. Add to prevent sticking. The cooking water can be used for a gravy, soup or sauce.
POTATOES that tend to discolour after boiling add 1 dessertspoonful of vinegar or lemon juice to every pint of water 10 minutes before the end of cooking.
POTATOES steamed or cooked in a pressure cooker, especially if cooked in their skins, retain more of the vitamin C content.
POTATOES should be served immediately to preserve the vitamin C.

Boiled New Potatoes

1 lb potatoes, scrubbed or scraped
1 teaspoon salt
Boiling water

METHOD
Place the potatoes and salt into a pan and barely cover with boiling water.
Place the lid on the pan and boil gently until cooked, about 15-20 minutes according to size.
Drain Well. Toss in butter if desired.

Boiled Potatoes
(Maincrop)

1 lb potatoes, peeled
1 teaspoon salt
Water

METHOD
Place the potatoes and salt into a pan and barely cover with cold water. Place the lid on the pan and bring to the boil. Reduce the heat and simmer the potatoes until cooked. Drain and dry over a low heat with the lid of the pan tilted.

Mashed Potatoes

1 lb potatoes, boiled
1 oz butter
1 tablespoon hot milk
Pepper

METHOD
Mash the potatoes thoroughly. Add the butter, milk and pepper to taste. Beat with a wooden spoon until fluffy.

Roast Potatoes

1 lb. potatoes, peeled
Salt and pepper
Oil or fat

METHOD
Cut potatoes into even sized pieces and dry.
Pour sufficient oil or fat into a roasting pan and place in the oven to heat the fat.
Remove and add the potatoes, dust with salt and pepper.
Return to the oven and cook at 425°F (220°C) Gas No. 7, basting occasionally with the fat until cooked, crisp and golden brown.
Drain.

Chipped Potatoes

1 lb potatoes, peeled
Oil or lard

METHOD
Cut the potatoes into ½″ (1 cm) fingers and place in a bowl of ice cold water for about 10 minutes.
Drain and dry thoroughly.
Place the fat into a deep pan (you will require 1½ pints (825ml) of oil for ½ lb (225g) chips in an 8″ (20 cm) standard chip pan) and heat to 375°F (190°C) or until a piece of bread will brown on one side in 30 seconds.
Place the chips into a frying basket and lower gently into the oil and cook for 3 minutes. Remove basket and allow the fat to reheat to 375°F (190°C) and cook the chips for a further 5 minutes until crisp and golden brown.

Sauté Potatoes

1 lb potatoes
2 oz butter or oil

METHOD
Peel the potatoes thinly and parboil in salted water for about 10 minutes. Drain well and dry off in the pan over a low heat. Cut the potatoes into ¼ inch thick slices.
Heat the butter or cooking oil in a frying pan, add the potatoes and fry on both sides until crisp and brown. (Approximately 10 minutes).

43 OTHER WAYS WITH POTATOES

For the basic cooking techniques turn to page 91
Quantities quoted below relate to 1 lb raw potatoes. Add salt and pepper to taste.

WAYS WITH BOILED POTATOES

1.   Cheese Chips. Parboil potatoes for 5 mins. Allow to cool slightly. Cut into chips and immediately place in melted butter, and coat with grated cheese. Place in buttered oven dish and bake until golden.

2.   Country-Style. Mix cubed raw potatoes with 4 oz. sliced button mushrooms. Simmer for ½ hour in ½ pint water with chicken stock cube. Add 2 oz. butter, 1 teasp. lemon juice and a pinch of cayenne pepper. Sprinkle with chopped parsley before serving.

3.   Mâitre d'Hôtel. Parboil the potatoes for 5 mins. Allow to cool slightly, then slice as thinly as possible. Place in a shallow dish and cover with 1 pint milk and stock (½ milk to ½ stock). Add salt and pepper, and slice onion over the top. Bring to boil gently over slow heat and simmer until potatoes are tender. Strain before serving. Serve hot, using the milky stock as a sauce.

4.   Nanette. Wash and scrape new potatoes and leave in cold water until required. Melt 1 oz. butter in a saucepan, add 2 tablesp. flour and stir well until brown. Add 1 pint stock slowly, stirring all the time. Add salt and a pinch of nutmeg, Bring gently to the boil, add potatoes and two sprigs parsley. Cover the saucepan and cook very slowly until tender. Serve hot.

5.   Peppered. Sliced raw potatoes and a sliced onion. Simmer for 10 mins. Meanwhile slice a small green pepper (discarding the core and seeds), blanch by leaving in boiling water for 3 mins., drain and add to potatoes. Mix with 2 tablesp. tomato sauce and cook for 10 mins.

6.   Punch Nep. Sliced raw potatoes and 1 lb. turnips with ½ lb. sliced onions. Fry lightly. Add ¼ pint water, with ½ a beef stock cube, and simmer for ½ hour till water is absorbed. Mash. (Add cream if desired).

7.   Devilled. New potatoes boiled and sliced into a hot sauce (1 oz. butter, 1 teasp. made mustard, 1 tablesp. vinegar, and a pinch of cayenne pepper cooked together for 2 minutes).

WAYS WITH MASHED POTATOES

8.   Berny. Add 1 egg, 1 oz. butter, mix well together. Shape into balls. coat with beaten egg, then chopped almonds, and fry in deep fat.

9.   Creamy Cheese. Chop and mix in a packet (3 oz.) of soft cheese over heat until the cheese melts and blends. Add chopped parsley and chives (or spring onions).

10.   Devilled Potatoes. Boil and sieve or rice potatoes. Add freshly ground black pepper and cayenne to taste. When cool, shape into flat, round biscuits ½" thick. Fry gently in hot fat. Serve with curries.

11.   Duchesse. Mix in a beaten egg and 1 oz. butter, put into a forcing bag with a No. 10 star nozzle and pipe into swirls on a greased baking sheet. Bake (425°F, Mark 7) until lightly browned (about 15 mins.), brushing the top with a little beaten egg when half done. Duchesse potato can be piped round fish and meat dishes.

12.   Hash Brown. Spread all over a frypan greased with butter or bacon fat, and leave till brown underneath (about 10 mins.). Fold over with a slice and slide on to a plate. (Any of the following can be mixed in: cooked mushrooms, bacon, onion, tomato, grated cheese).

13.   Lorette. Boil or steam the potatoes and sieve or rice them. Add salt and pepper, and allow to cool. Beat 1 egg into the mashed potato until a smooth texture results. Next, shape the mixture into crescents or half-moons. Drop into hot fat and fry until light golden-brown. Serve hot or cold.

14.   Miroton. Boil or steam the potatoes and sieve or rice. Chop an onion and fry in 2 oz. butter until pale golden-brown. Add the potatoes, stir in 1 tablesp. ketchup or chutney and two beaten eggs. Add salt and pepper. Lightly butter an oven dish and sprinkle the inside with breadcrumbs. Fill with the preparation and bake in a moderate oven for 30 mins.

15.   Oaties. Mix with 6 oz. porridge oats and a little milk. Roll this dough out on a floured board till ⅛" thick. Prick with a fork, cut out into rounds or triangles, and bake quickly on a greased griddle or thick frypan. Serve with butter.

16.   Potato and Apple Purée. Boil, drain and mash potatoes, and add to purée of cooking apples. Mix together. Add sugar, salt and pepper to taste. Use ⅔ potato to ⅓ apple purée.

17.   Rotmos. Mix together equal quantities of mashed potatoes and swede. Add 2 oz. melted butter, salt and pepper.

18.   Stelk. Cook a small bunch of spring onions in milk till tender and mix both onions and milk into the mashed potato. Beat till fluffy, pile in mounds on plates, making a well in the centre of each mound for a lump of butter. The stelk is eaten from the outside, each forkful being dipped into the melting butter. This is a traditional country dish and a good way to use old potatoes which tend to smash.

WAYS WITH SAUTÉ POTATOES

19.   Browned. Use tiny, whole new potatoes. Cook in shallow fat, turning often until golden-brown and crisp.

20.   Corn Tricks. Grate the raw potatoes, pour off surplus water, and add 2 oz. flour, 2 beaten eggs, 8 oz. can of sweet corn kernels, 2 tablesp. milk. Fry tablespoonfuls until golden, turning half way through.

21.   Creole. With potato slices, fry large sliced onion (use low heat, for about 35 mins. — or until onions are tender), turning frequently. Spread 2 tablesp. tomato sauce over and cook for a further 10 mins.

22.   Herbies. When the potato slices are half fried, sprinkle with 2 tablesp. packet stuffing; keep turning until browned.

23. Peasant Potatoes. Cut potatoes into small cubes. Peel and crush 1 clove garlic. Fry potato and garlic in mixture of butter and oil. Before serving, sprinkle with chopped parsley if desired.

24. Soured. To the potato slices add 1 tablesp. chopped chives and ¼ pint carton of soured cream (or yoghourt). Simmer till cream is absorbed.

25. Potatoes Limousine. Grate potatoes coarsely, mix with small cubes of fat bacon. Season well. Heat fat in frying-pan, spread mixture evenly over pan and fry until golden brown on both sides.

26. Potatoes Sablées. These 'sandy' potatoes, as their name betrays, are cut in dice when raw, then fried slowly in butter, some fine breadcrumbs being added towards the end.

27. Sweet Brown. Use tiny, whole, new potatoes. Turn them in syrup (1 oz. butter and 1 oz. sugar) in a frypan until browned.

28. Tartan Crispots. Use tiny, whole, new potatoes. After boiling toss in melted butter and then porridge oats. Fry till crisp.

WAYS WITH
FRIED POTATOES

29. Batter Potatoes. Cut potatoes into quarters. Boil carefully for 5-7 mins. Drain and dry carefully; dip in a frying batter. Deep-fry until golden.

30. Curls. Continue to peel the peeled potatoes, and put the strips to soak for half an hour. Dry on kitchen paper. Fry till crisp.

31. Julienne. Peel potatoes and wash them thoroughly in running water. Cut into slivers resembling matchsticks, then wash again in running cold water. Drain well, place in frying basket and immerse in hot fat for 3-4 mins. Sprinkle with salt. Serve hot or cold as garnish or cocktail savoury.

32. King Scout. Parboil potatoes. Allow to cool slightly and then slice ¼" thick. Dust well on both sides with pepper and salt. Prepare a batter with 4 oz. flour, 1 egg and a little water. Dip potato slices in batter and then into hot, deep fat. Fry until golden brown. Remove and drain well. Serve hot, garnished with parsley.

33. Soufflé Potatoes. Peel and trim potatoes into squares. Cut into slices ⅛" thick. Rinse and place in ice-cold water for at least ½ hour. Dry them and blanch in moderately hot fat, for 2 or 3 mins. Drain. Reheat fat to 390°F. Immerse potatoes in fat until they puff out like little balloons, Dry and drain on kitchen paper. Sprinkle with a very little salt and serve immediately.

WAYS WITH
ROAST AND
BAKED POTATOES

34. Baked/Roast. This is a cross between the two methods. Scrub and dry large or medium unpeeled potatoes, melt 1 oz. butter in a roasting tin, and bake, with cut side down (400°F. Mark 6) for 30-40 mins. or until tender.

35. Boston Roast Potatoes. Peel and cover with cold water, bring to boil and simmer for 5 mins. Drain and when cool enough to handle, score the surface of the potatoes with prongs of a fork. Dip in melted fat and place around the roast for about 1-1¼ hours, basting occasionally. To serve, sprinkle with a little salt.

36. Dauphinoise. Butter an ovenproof dish that has been rubbed with garlic (optional). Put in alternate layers of raw, ⅛" thick, sliced potatoes and 3 oz. grated cheese, finishing with cheese. Beat 1 egg in ½ pint milk, with nutmeg, then pour over. Bake (375°F. Mark 5) for 1-1½ hours, until brown.

37. Delicious. Put the sliced raw potatoes on a large sheet of aluminium foil with ¼ pint carton double cream and 2 oz. grated cheese. Make a secure parcel, put in a baking tin and bake (400°F, Mark 6) for about an hour or until soft

38. Foiled. Wrap tiny, raw, new potatoes with butter and mint in an aluminium foil parcel and place on a baking sheet. Bake (350°F, Mark 4) for 30-45 mins.

39. Newport Roast Potatoes. Parboil potatoes for 3 mins. Drain, dry, roll in well-seasoned flour. Roast for 1½ hours around joint, basting frequently with hot fat.

40. Normandie. Dice potatoes into small cubes and moisten with 2 tablesp. milk. Chop 1 small onion and 1 small leek and fry together in butter. Add the potatoes. Season well and bake in moderate oven for 40-50 mins. Serve with fish.

41. Scalloped. Butter an ovenproof dish and put in sliced raw potatoes, covered with 1 large chopped onion. Top with 1 oz. white breadcrumbs and 2 oz. melted butter. Bake (375°F, Mark 5) for 1-1½ hours or until soft.

42. Tropical. Slice boiled new potatoes and add a small tin of pineapple chunks in a shallow ovenproof dish. Pour 1 oz. melted butter and 1 oz. brown sugar over. Bake (400°F, Mark 6) for 20 mins. or brown under the grill.

43. Viennese. Wash potatoes thoroughly and steam in their skins. Peel while still hot. Slice thickly and arrange in alternate layers with 1 lb sliced tomatoes in a buttered oven dish, season each layer and pour over a little cream. Cover the top layer with breadcrumbs and dot with a little butter. Bake in a moderate oven for 30 mins. Serve hot in oven dish, as an accompaniment to baked or fried fish.

METRIC MEASUREMENT EQUIVALENTS

Although many items are now sold by Metric weight or liquid **measure** most housewives still prefer to cook using the Imperial system. In this book no metric equivalents have been shown in the recipes but for those who are metrically minded here are some useful tables for making conversions.

DRY WEIGHT	
Imperial Ounce (oz)	**Recommended gram (g) conversion to nearest 25g**
1	25 (28)
2	50 (57)
3	75 (85)
4 (¼ lb)	125 (113)
5	150 (142)
6	175 (170)
7	200 (198)
8 (½ lb)	225 (227)
9	250 (255)
10	275 (284)
11	300 (311)
12 (¾ lb)	350 (340)
13	375 (368)
14	400 (396)
15	425 (425)
16 (1 lb)	450 (453)

LIQUID MEASURES		
Imperial fluid Ounce (fl oz)	**Imperial Pint**	**Recommended Millilitre equivalent**
20	1	600 (568)
10	½	300 (284)
5	¼	150 (142)

Note

Mixing Metric and Imperial measures is not recommended. In cake making the slight differences become critical and even in other recipes the results are often far from satisfactory.

Thrush

INDEX

The recipes indexed below are in sections according to the principal ingredient.

Photo by Richard Cox

Hedgehog